RUTH

Book of Ruth Commentary

William R. Doolin, B.D., Th.M.

TRUSTHOUSE
PUBLISHERS

Copyright © 2019, William R. Doolin B.D

Book of Ruth Commentary

All Scripture quotations are from the King James Holy Bible unless otherwise noted. Any deviations from the text were not intended. Please accept my apologies for any such errors.

ISBN: 978-1-945774-31-7

Trust House Publishers
P.O.Box 3181
Taos, NM 87571

www.trusthousepublishers.com

Ordering Information: Special discounts are available on quantity purchases by churches, associations, and retailers. For details, contact the publisher at the address above or call toll-free 1-844-321-4202.

1 2 3 4 5 6 7 8 9

First and foremost, I would like to dedicate this work to my Lord and Saviour Jesus Christ. I would also like to show my appreciation to my mother and daughter by dedicating this work to them secondarily. I thank my mother for helping to lead me to the Lord as a child, supporting all my endeavors my entire life, helping me to raise my children and administrating the business that the Lord blessed us with, thus making it possible to for me to get a biblical education to better serve the Lord. (2 Tim. 1:5; 3:15). My daughter has been one of the best blessings in my life outside of having a saving knowledge of, and relationship with the Lord Jesus Christ. My daughter has prayed for me, comforted me, lifted me up many times and has been very accommodating with my service to the Lord. She has been an excellent daughter and servant of the Lord, saving me from much grief that would have ensued if not for her warm relationship with our Saviour. Without the inspiration and help of these two great women in my life, it is very likely I would not have been able to get this far in my ministry (Col. 4:17)!

Table of Contents

Appreciation 1

Acknowledgment 3

Introduction to Book of Ruth 5

Chapter 1: Ruth does not waiver 11

Chapter 2: Ruth goes to work 49

Chapter 3: Ruth wows and waits 83

Chapter 4: Ruth gets wedded 101

Bibliography 115

APPRECIATION

I would like to also state my sincere and deepest appreciation for the examples shown to me by my instructors, pastors, friends who heeded the call from God in their lives, and me being one of the fruit that was produced by their faithfulness to that calling. These people provided me with direction, inspiration, forgiveness, superior instruction and example in my walk with the Lord. Dr. Peter S. Ruckman, Dr. Brian Donovan, Chaplain Ted Warmack D.D., Dr. David Peacock, Dr. David Walker, Dr. Greg Estep, Bro. Mike Wheeler, Bro. Sam Magdalein, and all the faculty and staff at The Bible Doctrine Institute and Charity Bible Baptist College respectively.

ACKNOWLEDGMENT

I acknowledge that I was a hell bound sinner who had no use for God and was not interested in serving Him, much less reading His Holy Bible. The Lord saw fit to save this poor sinner and did not stop His work there-to my amazement!

Without the mercy and grace of our Lord, I would have died alone, having no hope, without God and gone straight to hell (Eph. 2:12).

The Lord allowed me to be saved with a King James Bible (1 Pet. 1:23) rather than a faulty translation by putting me in the path of a "Ruckmanite". After that, the Lord called me to preach and gave me an education that I did not deserve teaching me correct biblical doctrine rightly divided. (2 Tim. 3:16, 2 Tim. 2:15). The Lord then opened doors for me in 2009 to serve in jail, nursing home and street ministries for his glory of which I am so grateful.

I thank the Lord for the strength to complete this commentary, having clarity of mind and bringing all things to my remembrance that I have heard, read and studied for this work (Phil. 4:13, John 14:26).

(Rev. 4:11) Thou art worthy, O Lord, to receive glory and honour and power: for thou hast created all things, and for thy pleasure they are and were created. Amen.

INTRODUCTION TO BOOK OF RUTH

The book of Ruth, along with the book of Esther are the only two books in the bible that bear a woman's name, the writer is anonymous. It is the author's belief, that although there are many offerings as to who the writer may have been, is not as important as the historical, doctrinal and spiritual content that is contained therein.

The events of Ruth take place in the Old Testament during the time of the book of Judges ranging from 1322 B.C. to 1186 B.C. during the fourth of thirteen famines in the Bible. The book has 4 chapters, 85 verses, and 2,574 words. The book is included in the historical section of the Kethubim which Christ referred to as the Psalms (Luke 24:44) according to Dr. Peter Ruckman.[1]

Some scholars like Edward F. Campbell, classify the book of Ruth as just a story[2]; like the book of Jonah or even the second advent, however, this is no surprise to the Bible believer versed in the standard operating procedure of the Alexandrian Cult. Anything that can be spiritualized will

---
1 Ruckman, Peter S. Judges and Ruth Commentary. BB Bookstore, 2015, p. 326.
2 Campbell, Edward F. Jr. Ruth. Doubleday & Company, Inc., 1975, pp. 3-4.

be, to take away the significance of God's words and ultimately diminish one's faith in the Holy Bible. (Gen. 3:1).

Dr. Greg Estep [3] stated, The Lord spent more time talking to a Samaritan woman who was married, divorced and remarried than He did talking to the leaders in Israel at that time like Nicodemus. The Lord did this because the Samaritan woman was looking for the truth and when a person is searching for the truth, the Lord is obligated to send it (Rom. 2:6-9) cf. Ethiopian Eunuch (Acts 9), Cornelius (Acts 10) who were seeking God. If a person is not looking for the truth, then God will send them a lie. (Ezek. 14:1-5, 1 Kings 22:22, Heb. 4:12-13). You get out of the Bible what you put in!

The IMPORTANCE of the book of Ruth is that it traces the genealogy of the Messiah, while containing significant typology and prophetical material (2 Pet. 1:20). Ruth-a Gentile, after the death of her Jewish husband, follows her mother in law Naomi back to her people (the Jews) and receives blessings from the Lord (Gen. 12:3). In typology, this illustrates Christ taking His Gentile bride (Eph. 2:11-19; Rev. 19). A type is not a parable, or a story, nor figurative language as some claim the book of Ruth to be. A type is "in the science of theology it properly signifies the preordained representative relation which certain persons events and institutions of the OT bare to corresponding persons events and institutions in the NT, or which effectively prefigures some truth connected with Christianity".[4] In simpler terms a type is a pattern, shadow, or figure of things to come; so, Ruth is not a story but recorded history.

Ruth chronicles the events of an unsaved hell bound idol worshipping woman who follows a Jew to salvation and is greatly blessed by the Lord. Because of her humble spirit and her willingness to sacrifice, surrender,

---

3 Estep, Greg. MD5078 Ruth. (CBBI Audio Tape 10 vs19@118 minutes).

4 Hauenstein, Michael. MD5082 Typology. (CBBI Audio Tape 1@12 minutes approx.).

submit, and serve, the Lord blesses Ruth with the right husband at the right time according to God's providence. The Book of Esther, a counterpart to Ruth, does not mention God but clearly shows Him working behind the scenes. In Ruth, God and Lord appear throughout the text and His providence is manifested.[5] Ruth is delivered from her affliction, double typing a Gentile being saved in the tribulation and being a type of the bride of Christ. Ruth gets blessed, goes from famine to feast and has her name recorded in the Bible for all eternity (Ps. 119:89).

Prophetically, the book of Ruth reveals the bride of Christ, a Gentile, which was not known in the Old Testament, nor during the times of the gospels but was later revealed to the apostle Paul (Gal.1; Eph. 2). Ruth also contains a type of the Rapture (Ch. 3:8), demonstrates God's providence in (Ch. 2:3), as previously stated, and pictures God's redemption in the near kinsman redeemer of Boaz (Ch. 2:1).

Main Characters:

1. Ruth: Gentile bride of Christ in type, she is a Gentile Moabitess whose lineage if from Lot and his incestuous relationship with his daughters (Gen. 19:37-38). Moab means "water of a father" or "desire".[6] Ruth lived in Moab and worshipped false gods such as Molech and Chemosh. Her people, the Moabites, were enemies to the Jews because they did not let Israel pass through their land during the wilderness journey nor give them bread and water, so God dealt bitterly with them. The Moabites also hired Baalim unsuccessfully to curse the Jews (Deut. 23:4). God calls Moab His "washpot" (Ps. 60:8; 108:9). When the children of Israel entered the land of Canaan, they were to leave Moab alone and not mix with them (Deut. 2:9). Ruth appears in the

---

5 (Ruckman Ruth Commentary 325).
6 abarim-publications.com/Meaning/Moab.html#.Ww4LjyAh2Uk.

Bible in the following verses: (Ruth 1:4,14,16,22; 2:2,8,21,22; 3:9; 4:5,10,13; Matt. 1:5).

2. Elimelech: Jews in the tribulation, a Jew who fled from the famine in Israel to save his flesh and was out of the Lord's will for his life; which he paid for with his death (Rom. 8:13). Elimelech appears in the Bible in the following verses: (Ruth 1:2,3; 2:1,3; 4:3,9).

3. Naomi: Israel in type. Elimelech's wife, who subserviently and in subjection, followed her husband out of the house of bread into Moab, losing both of her sons and her husband. She wanted to be called Mara=bitter, because the Lord had dealt bitterly with her in these losses. Naomi appears in the Bible in the following verses: (Ruth 1:2,3,8,11,19,20,21,22; 2:1,2,6,20,22;3:1;4:3,5,9,14,16,17).

4. Mahlon: Elimelech and Naomi's son who married a Moabite- Ruth and died. Mahlon appears in the Bible in the following verses: (Ruth 1:2,5;4:9,10).

5. Chilion: Elimelech and Naomi's son who married a Moabite- Orpah and died. Chilion appears in the Bible in the following verses: (Ruth 1:2,5; 4:9).

6. Boaz: Jesus in type. Boaz is the main character who figures Christ purchasing the Church by redeeming and marrying Ruth, the wealthy kinsman redeemer suppling all our needs (Phil. 4:19). Boaz appears in the Bible in the following verses: (Ruth 2:1,3,4,5,8,11,14,15,19,23; 3:27; 4:1,5,8,9,13; 1 Kings 7:21; 1 Chron.2:11,12; 3;17).

Let us remember that when rightly dividing the word (2 Tim. 2:15), "we must ask who is speaking", "what is being said," and "who is being spoken to"? Every verse of scripture has historical, doctrinal and spiritual/devotional applications to the believer. (1 Cor. 2:13).

Even though Ruth is an Old Testament book written in the days "when there was no king in Israel: every man did that which was right in his own eyes" (Judg. 21:25) and before the New Testament had been affected (Matt. 27:52; Heb. 9:16) the book contains one of the greatest love stories in the Bible and is applicable to the modern Christian.

Ruth is a book that has a lot of gleaning to be done to edify the body of Christ (Ch. 2:19). The book is replete with examples of God's patience, providence, redemption, His nature to work and provide, God's welfare system, seeking the perfect will of the Lord, rather than just settling for the good or acceptable, trusting in the Lord, and has numerous typology examples, contains prophecy, and has a happy ending!

CHAPTER ONE

---◆◆◆---

RUTH DOES NOT WAIVER

1:1 Now it came to pass in the days when the judges ruled, that there was a famine in the land. And a certain man of Bethlehemjudah went to sojourn in the country of Moab, he, and his wife, and his two sons.

"**Now it came to pass**" This is not a parable or a story. The Book of Ruth is a true historical account of Ruth traveling from Moab to Bethlehem to be *one* of the four Gentile women in the Messianic line- Ruth (Ruth 1:22), Tamar (Matt. 1:3), Rahab (Matt. 1:5), Rehoboam's mother (Matt. 1:7).

"**The days when the judges ruled**" Ruth takes place during the time of the judges between Ch. 3-4 at the time of Shamgar according to Usher and most chronologists.[7]

"**Famine**" This is the fourth of 13 famines listed in the Bible (1) Gen. 12:10, (2) Gen. 26:1, (3) Gen. 41:54-57, (4) here 1:1, (5) 2 Sam. 21:1, (6) 1 Kings 18:2, (7) 2 Kings 6:25, (8) 2 Kings 8:1, (9) 2 Kings 25:3, (10) Amos 8:11, (11) Acts 11:27-30, (12) Rev. 6:6-8, and (13) Rev. 18:8.

---

7   Canne, Browne, Blayney, Scott and others. The Treasury of Scripture Knowledge. MacDonald Publishing Company, 1982, p. 188.

Dearth[8] also is a synonym of famine and appears many times in the Bible. Dearth minus "d" is earth and dearth minus "r" is death. Famines are equated with death. Spiritually there is a famine/dearth in the land today for the word of God (Amos 8:11) and some Christians have replaced the KJV Bible with its blessings and advanced revelation to go into the world (Alexandria, Egypt) to a satanic counterfeit dead book-which is not a! God has a Bible (published by the Holy Spirit), church, music, and miracles. Satan has Bible a book (published by the "Yea hath God said society"), church, music, and miracles to imitate God (2 Thess. 2:8-10).

By taking prayer out of public school, the Ten Commandments out of the courthouse, making abortion and same-sex marriage legal, not preaching the seven mysteries given to the Apostle Paul, and having over four hundred translations of the Bible, which contain lies, makes Jesus a sinner for getting angry (N.I.V. Matt. 5:22), makes Mary a young woman instead of a virgin (R.S.V. Isa. 7:14), takes away the blood from the atonement (Good News for Modern Man Rev. 1:5), etc. we are starving for sound biblical doctrine. (2 Tim. 4:3-4). The N.I.V. version alone omits over 64,000 words from the text making it a "less calorie" or "lite" version of the Bible and when it comes to spiritual food, we need all the calories we can get (1 Sam. 3:19)!

"A certain man" This man has a name; Elimelech. Parables do not have names and so again this is not a parable or story, but just as real as the account of a beggar named Lazarus. (Luke 16:20).

"Bethlehemjudah went to sojourn in the country of Moab" Bethlehem means "house of bread". Bethlehem is important because this is where the bread of life entered the world (Mic 5:2 cf. John 6:35,48). Judah means "praising God". Elimelech left his land where he was commanded to

---

8 Webster, Noah. Webster's Dictionary 1828. webstersdictionary1828.com/Dictionary/dearth.

live and get blessed by the Lord (Deut. 5:33, 12:5), to go into the world to satisfy his flesh. "Yea, all that a man hath will he give for his life" (Job 2:4). There is no life in the world, just existence. Moab was cursed by God, so Elimelech had no business going there (Deut. 23:1-4)! Elimelech apparently did not trust God to meet his needs and so he trusted the arm of his flesh instead (Jer. 17:5). Further, God called Israel from the world unto Himself (Deut. 14:2), dealt with Israel as His chosen children, revealed Himself unto them like no other nation (Ps. 147:20) and gave Israel the oracles of God (Rom. 3:2).

God did not want Israel mixing with other nations because He knew they would leave Him and settle for their gods (Deut. 7:3). Baalim understood the way to destroy Israel was to get them to mix with the people of Moab and bring a curse upon them from God. Elimelech knew this from the law, so he tempted God by moving to Moab. Elimelech did not have abundance in Moab, just existed poorly until he died (John 10:10). In the Orient, a man's greatness in life is attested to by how many people attend his funeral; how many people came to Elimelech, Mahlon, and Chilion's funeral?

The spiritual application is that God does not want His children going to the World to meet their needs. For example, God forbade Solomon to go to Egypt-a type of the world-to buy horses, so why would you want a Bible from there or to live in the world like Elimelech did (Deut. 17:16)? God called His son out of Egypt, a type of the Rapture leaving this world (Matt. 2), called Jacob out (Gen. 49), Israel out in (Exod. 15), and even the bones of Joseph (Exod. 13). Soon the Lord will call the Church out of the world (1 Thess. 4:16-18).

Further, Christians were first called Christians at Antioch, Syria where the Textus Receptus originates vs. all the faulty translations that come from Alexandria, Egypt.⁹ Finally, Paul met his demise sailing to Italy on a ship from Alexandria, Egypt (Acts 27:6). If that were not enough, after that ship wrecked (Acts 27:41), Satan sent another ship from Alexandria whose sign was Castor and Pollux (Acts 28:11). The World will bring you to death (1 John 2:15-17). Also, Abraham got into trouble in Egypt lying about his wife and almost lost her to Pharaoh and took Hagar (Gen. 16) to wife, who is the mother of Ishmael. This is where the problem stems from today between the Jews and Arabs.¹⁰ GOD DOES NOT WANT A CHRISTIAN IN THE WORLD OR TO FOOL WITH IT!

2 And the name of the man *was* Elimelech, and the name of his wife Naomi, and the name of his two sons Mahlon and Chilion, Ephrathites of Bethlehem-judah. And they came into the country of Moab, and continued there.

"**Elimelech**" means "God is his King" Elimelech, like Esau's king, is his flesh (Gen. 25:32). Elimelech and Esau hungered for the things of the World more than communion with God. When the famine arose, instead of trusting the Lord, Elimelech ran to the World to meet his fleshly needs and missed the blessings of God, consequently suffering the deaths of his sons for being out of the will of God.

A Christian should not have to run to their wallet, neighbor, education, the manager, their mommy or any other substitute for the Lord. Trusting God means looking beyond what we can see to what God sees (Heb. 11:1). When you are in the world and out of church (or the land like Elimelech), you miss a blessing. The very day that you missed church is the day that the Lord was going to answer that question that you had

---

9 Ruckman, Peter S. The Christian's Handbook of Manuscript Evidence. Pensacola Bible Press. 1970, p. 38.

10 (Ruckman Ruth Commentary 337).

been asking of Him for so long, or show you some spiritual nugget in His word, or even have your favorite special sung but you missed it!

Your walk with the Lord is like a train ride. Once saved, you board the train. Every time you sin, you get off the train. The train keeps going. You can get back on the train by applying the blood (1 John 1:9) but each time you board the train, you will be in a different seat on the train from where you were before and will miss your original destination only to arrive somewhere else. A train has the most freedom when on its tracks; it can go anywhere then. If you take the train off its tracks and put it in the grass-because it does not want to be confined anymore and wants its freedom-then it has freedom but can not go anywhere because it was made to stay on the tracks.

We are made to glorify our Creator, not meet the needs of our flesh (Rev. 4:11). Elimelech represents, in type, a Jew in the tribulation who was disobedient. Obedience always brings a blessing (1 Sam. 15:22). Elimelech should have obeyed God and left all the consequences to Him instead of going to Moab. God's Word is an unmovable anchor in times of storm or famine, but Elimelech left the Lord. God does not require us to understand his will-just to obey it-even if it seems unreasonable such as starving in a famine. Anyway, the dark moments and famines of our life will last only so long as is necessary for God to accomplish His purpose in us.

Once Elimelech arrived in Moab, he never left. He did not intend to stay, but was consumed by the temporary (as Lot was), and lost sight of the eternal. L.S.D.:Look, Sin, Death. Many times, when I am preaching at the jail, sometimes an inmate will get his turn in the phone line, or his turn to use the washer or shower, or even his turn at the card table. They leave Bible study and usually never come back-even if they intended to-they get distracted. Satan showed Jesus all the kingdoms of the world-in a moment of time (Luke 4:5). Moses esteemed the reproach of Christ greater than enjoying the pleasure of sin for a season (Heb. 11:25). Jesus and Moses did not get distracted. Whatever is gained outside the will of God, eventually turns to ashes (1 Cor. 3:15); for Elimelech, this was literal (Gen. 3:19; Rom.6:23).

"Naomi" pictures Israel (in type), and her name means "full of pleasantries". Life was pleasant in Bethlehem, now she wants to be called "Mara" (vs.20) which means "bitterness". Peace with God, is the fruit of oneness with God but Naomi became bitter. When life treats you bad, remember how it treated Jesus. Being away from the Lord will make you bitter; the way of the transgressor has made Naomi hard (Prov. 13:15). Life has taken its toll on Naomi; however, she fares better than Elimelech as she returns after the tribulation to her land and sees Ruth enter the Messianic line, become the great grandmother to King David, and an ancestor to Jesus Christ. This blessing may have had to do with her being in subjection to her husband by following him to Moab and not rebelling against this poor and sinful decision, (1 Pet. 3:6); although once her husband died, she should have returned to Bethlehem immediately, as she was no longer under bondage. However, upon Naomi's return (just as the Prodigal son) she is blessed (Ruth 4:16).

"Mahlon and Chilion" Mahlon means "sickly" and Chilion means "pinning".[11] It is amazing how, in the Bible, the Lord will name people and places before they are born or relevant and then bring to pass in history events that coincide accurately with the names down to the scruple! Israel was far away from the Lord and sick from sin when Jesus came; Mahlon and Chilion were far away from Bethlehem, thus sick as well. Both children end up marrying women who worship idols, cause them to sin (1 Kings 11:1)

---

11 (Ruckman Ruth Commentary 337).

against the law (Deut. 7:3-4) and get them deeper into the World making it harder to return home. They stay in the world, get sick, and ultimately pay for their sin with their lives (1 Cor. 11:30; 1 John 5:16).

3 And Elimelech Naomi's husband died; and she was left, and her two sons.

"died" Elimelech went to sojourn "a temporary stay"[12] in the land of his enemies, but ended up dying there separated from God, alone with only his family, in the World and without hope (Eph. 2:12). Anything you hold too tightly, you will lose. Elimelech lost it all to gain the world-Moab (Mark 8:36). "Sin will always take you further than you wanted to go, keep you longer than you wanted to stay, and cost you more than you wanted to pay".[13]

Many years ago, I knew of a musician (Bradley Nowell, lead singer of a music group called Sublime) who wanted to "spark his creativity", so he made a plan to use (sojourn) drugs for five years; he called it the five-year plan. At the end, he would be rich, famous and stop using drugs, because the drugs were just the vehicle get him to fame. He had one musical hit (Santeria)-AFTER HE DIED-leaving behind a spouse and children; this was not his original intention! He was not going to stay, he was just passing through to become a star, but the temporary became eternal!

David made the same mistake; running from Saul into the World to disappear off the radar/grid in order to save his flesh (1 Sam. 27:1). Disappointments are inevitable; discouragement is a choice! David chose to desert the same God who brought the lion, the bear, and Goliath into his hands-but feared Saul-like Elijah feared Jezebel (1 Kings 19:4). So, God chastened David with the lessons of Ziklag and broke him. Brokenness

---

12 (Ruckman Ruth Commentary 336).
13 (Ruckman Ruth Commentary 336).

is God's requirement for maximum usefulness. David repented, left the world, and returned to the Lord. David encouraged himself IN the Lord. (1 Sam. 30:6), ENQUIRED of the Lord (vs.8), and went IN pursuit with the Lord (vs. 10). David repented and went back to God, Elimelech died a nobody in his enemy's house and settled for crumbs-famine crumbs at that!

God acts on behalf of those who wait for him and all that Satan offers is crumbs for a moment of time (Luke 4:20). Rudiments of the world that have you settling for crumbs: "One drink is too many and a thousand is not enough", "I can quit anytime I want", "Everyone else is doing it", "No one will know", "A little can't hurt", "You gotta make a living", "It all depends on how you look at it". But, a little leaven, leaveneth the whole lump (Gal. 5:9). All unrighteousness is sin (1 John 5:17), so a Christian must ask himself: 1. Do I want to be doing or saying this when the Lord comes? 2. Does it edify anybody? 3. Does it get you under its power? All things are lawful but not expedient (1 Cor. 6:12; 10:23).

God assumes full responsibility for our needs when we obey Him. When we leave the Lord and go into the world, He is no longer obligated to protect and bless us, but many times He still does. The prophet of 1 Kings 13 only got one chance, where as Jonah had at least two-the free ride in the taxi cab-another up to date version!-being the second. David had the sure mercies and if God had to pay for my sins with His credit card, he would have had to contact the issuer for another card as the magnetic strip would be worn out!

There is only death or life, heaven or hell, God or the devil, black or white, up or down, saved or unsaved, etc. Elimelech **"died"** in his sin (Ezek. 18:26) because he got on his horse and left Israel instead of on his knees in Israel! If you fight all your battles on your knees, then you will win every time because a Christian stands tallest and strongest on their knees. Elimelech did not return to the Lord as David did, so he died.

"and she was left" cf. (Heb. 13:5-6). The Lord never leaves his child. No Christian has ever been called to "go it alone" in his or her walk of faith. With Elimelech's death, Naomi is free to return to Bethlehem but chooses to stay in Moab-it is hard to leave the world. Listening to God is essential to walking with God but she got comfortable in the world and continued in disobedience. Naomi was accepted there, no one was judgmental, and she became familiar with the sinful practices of the Moabites. They were not so bad (I mean we have to respect everyone's religion, right? We all worship the same God, right? There are many paths to heaven, right?).

Someone said "this book will keep you from your sins, or your sins will keep you from this book"! Sin affects those around us and Elimelech's sin has affected Naomi and his children cf. Achan's sin that affected his whole family (Josh. 7), and David's sin that affected his own family along with the whole nation of Israel (2 Sam. 12; 24:17). David reaped what he sowed, more than he sowed, later than he sowed, and had to pay back four lambs for his sin (Exod. 22:1). Lamb (1.) The baby died, (2 Sam. 12:18) which had to do with having sex with Bathsheba, person for person. Lamb (2.) Amnon was killed, (2 Sam. 13:29) which had to do with abandoning a man, so he would get killed. Lamb (3.) Absalom was killed, (2 Sam. 18:15) which had to do with getting killed during combat like Uriah. Lamb (4.) Amasa was killed (2 Sam. 20:10) which had to do with murder by a pretended friend.[14]

4 And they took them wives of the women of Moab; the name of the one *was* Orpah, and the name of the other Ruth: and they dwelled there about ten years.

---

14 Ruckman, Peter S. The Ruckman Reference Bible. BB Bookstore, 2009, p. 484.

"And they took them wives of the women of Moab" Naomi's refusal to go back to Bethlehem results in her two sons marrying "unsaved women", in type (Deut. 7:3; 23:3). It is not until the death of her two boys that she even considers going back to "the house of bread". Naomi has attended three funerals now. Her children have mixed with the world, but her heart is so hardened that she can not hear the Lord telling her to come home (Isa. 55).

"the name of the one *was* Orpah, and the name of the other Ruth" Orpah is mentioned first, with Ruth being mentioned second. The Bible contains "second" benefits, with the second turning out being better than the first; and God choosing the second over the first: (1.) In Adam-all die/ Christ-all live. (2.) Abel, Adam's second son, sheds a blood sacrifice that was better than Cain's sacrifice. Cain kills his younger brother Abel cf. Jesus is killed by his brethren. (3.) Noah had 3 sons (Gen. 10) Ham was younger, Japeth older, but Shem who is the second son gets the blessing from Noah. (4.) Jacob's son Ishmael is cast out but the blessing is given in Isaac the second son. (5.) Isaac has two sons. Jacob, the second, got both benefits-not Esau. (6.) Joseph when Jacob was dying, brought in his two sons to Jacob, but Jacob blessed the second younger son instead of the elder. (7.) Joseph was chosen over Reuben for the blessing. (8.) Moses was called and got the blessing, not Aaron. (9.) Moses's second set of the ten commandments were better than first because the first contained no offer of mercy or grace. (10.) The second Adam is better than the first (1 Cor.15:45). (11.) David was the second king after Saul, and a better king. (12.) The second birth (spiritual) is better than the first birth (physical). (13.) The second sometimes involves a translation which is better than the original cf. Enoch was better after he was translated. The kingdom was better after it was translated from Saul to David. The believer is better after translated from death to life (Col. 1:13-14).

Dr. Ruckman says "The King James Bible is better than the originals because no one has the originals, so you can not read them. The originals had no verse or paragraph markings to be able to locate a portion of scripture easily. The originals were written in uncial block letters that ran together so that the reader did not know if he had "abundanceonthetable", or "a bun dance on the table". The originals contained no advanced revelation like the King James Bible does. The originals did not produce as much fruit as the King James Bible, the majority of the world's population was converted under the King James Bible".[15]

There has come from the British and Foreign Bible Society, 1,000,000,000 King James Bibles. In 1904 they were putting out 32,876 copies a day (22 copies per minute). The American Bible Society produced 118,200,000 before 1945, which means at the present time there are-on this earth somewhere-1,118,200,000 English Bibles, and over 1,090,000,000 of them are Authorized Versions from 1611. This excludes the Bible printed and sold by Thomas Nelson and Sons, World Publishing Company, and others. The AV of 1611 will outnumber any five other English translations combined. This was done with the entire body of Conservative and Fundamental scholarship against it for more than one hundred years, and literally millions of dollars gone into the promotion of its corrupt competitors (RV, RSV, NRSV, ASV, NASV, NIV, NKJV, etc.).[16] So, the second (KJV) is better than the first (the originals).

"Orpah" Orpah means "neck" or "fawn".[17] Orpah is a type of a Gentile that does not get saved and loses her inheritance by staying in the world instead of going to Bethlehem, probably because she did not want to stick

---

15 Ruckman, Peter S. Psalms Commentary Vol. 2. BB Bookstore, 2002, pp. 1241-42.
16 (Ruckman pp. 1241-42).
17 biblehub.com/topical/o/orpah.htm.

her "neck" out for the Lord! **"Ruth"** Ruth means "friendship".[18] Ruth was a good friend to Naomi and Boaz.

"ten years" Usually people spend more time out of the will of God than in the will of God cf. Moses on the back side of the desert for forty years out of the will of God for committing murder (Exod. 2:15).

"Ten" is the number for Gentiles and Naomi is living among the Gentiles. Nebuchadnezzar's Image, and the Ten Horns of Daniels "fourth beast", that point to the Ten Kings, or Kingdoms, typified by the Ten Horns of John's "Beast" (Rev. 17:3,12), we see summing up the Gentile power in Ten Federated Kingdoms, which will be the completion of worldly Gentile rule, and which will be destroyed by the "Stone Kingdom" of Christ. Then we have the Ten "pieces of silver" (Lk. 15:8), and the Ten servants to whom were entrusted Ten pounds and one rewarded by being given authority over Ten cities (Luke 19:13,17) and the Ten plagues of Egypt.[19]

Gen. 10, the tower of Babylon, should be mentioned as well as the first Gentile ecumenical project. Further Solomon's reign pictures the millennial reign of the "Son of David" over the Gentiles (see especially Psa. 96:10-13; Zech. 14:9-21; Mal. 1:11; Acts 15:16-17. (sic)[20] Solomon's temple contained ten brazen lavers instead of one (1 Kings 7:27), ten candlesticks instead of one (2 Chron. 4:7), ten tables of shewbread instead of one (2 Chron. 4:8).

5 And Mahlon and Chilion died also both of them; and the woman was left of her two sons and her husband.

"died" In the bible, the number five represents death. Here in vs. 5 Mahlon and Chilion die, Adam dies at nine hundred and thirty years old

---

18 Strong, James. Strong's Exhaustive Concordance of the Bible. World Bible Publishers, Inc.1991, #7327, p. 142.
19 Larkin, Clarence. The Greatest Book on Dispensational Truth in the World. Rev. Clarence Larkin Est.1920, pp. 172-173.
20 (Ruckman Reference Bible 520).

in (Gen. 5:5). The word death has five letters as does Satan/devil, cross- where Jesus died is five letters, and Jesus had five wounds that resulted in His death.[21] Jesus name has five letters because He died for us. In (2 Sam. 2:23; 3:4,27; 4:6; 20:10), men die from being stabbed in the fifth rib. In Rev. the fifth seal poured by the fifth angel brings death, destruction or pain. (Rev. 6:9; 9:1; 16:10).

If necessary, God will move heaven and earth to show us His will. Like Job, the Lord has removed Naomi's immediate family to get her attention. Our intimacy with God-His highest priority for our lives-determines the impact of our lives. Naomi's life has been impacted tragically but adversity is a bridge to a deeper relationship with God. As a child of God, we are never victims of our circumstances and once we go to the Lord in prayer, the Lord will turn the problem into a profitable experience if we respond correctly (Rom 8:28).

Charles Stanley said in a sermon on the 23 Psalm during the 1990's, that the proper response when in times of difficulty is "(1.) Lord, here am I. (2.) How do you want me to respond to the circumstances that I am in? (3.) What is your goal for the circumstances that I am in? (4.) All that I have, I lay before your feet". I would like to take the devotional liberty to state that Naomi could have been in prayer here in vs. 5 and rose up from prayer in vs.6-I hope she prayed because that is where the solution begins. More likely though, Naomi after the funerals heard the famine was over and, again, made a decision to follow the food back to Bethlehem, still operating in the stubborn flesh.

6 Then she arose with her daughters in law, that she might return from the country of Moab: for she had heard in the country of Moab how that the LORD had visited his people in giving them bread.

---

21 (Ruckman Reference Bible 12).

"arose" "A Christian that rests, rusts", so you have to rise and get going if you want to serve the Lord and find out His will for your life. Jonah arose from his sleep after running from the Lord to find himself FACING perilous times (Jonah 3:3); Naomi is IN perilous times. The men of Nineveh are going to rise to condemn the generation that did not REPENT at the preaching of Jesus (Matt. 12:41), Naomi has not REPENTED but is hungry. The prodigal son, once he CAME to his senses, rose out of sin then returned to the Father (Luke 15:18). Naomi has not COME to her sense but has COME to the end of herself. Naomi is seeking the PROVISION at this point, not the PROVIDER. Baalim AROSE for the love of money (Num. 22:20; 1 Tim. 6:10); Naomi is RISING to satisfy her flesh. The beggar asking alms at the gate called Beautiful outside of the temple ROSE and walked because Peter had NO money (Acts 3:6). Naomi has NOTHING left; she departed home full and returns empty. If Jesus did not RISE from the dead, then we of all men would be most miserable (1 Cor. 15:19) and still be in darkness and famine.

If God had not visited His people, it is highly probable that Naomi would have died in Moab-in her sin-and gone to hell. The Syrians rose and fled to save their flesh, leaving all their goods to the lepers of 2 Kings 7, who decided not to sit around and die but to rise up and see what would happen. They arose and found the spoil of the Syrians provided by the Lord and the famine ended the next day. The point is, that sometimes we get ourselves into the "valley" (Ps.23) and the Lord will let us sojourn there as long as we like. How long we spend in the "valley", is entirely upon us and when we respond correctly, we will be lead out by the Good Shepherd. He will never let go of our hand, even though we let go of his (Footprint Poem), but when we are ready, He will lead us out of the "valley". Naomi is going home!

"the Lord had visited his people in giving them bread." Bread in the bible is likened to the word (John 6:35) and Jesus is likened to the word (John 1:1). We know that at the name of Jesus, every knee should bow and that it is a name above every name (Phil. 2:10-11). Further, the bible states that the word is magnified above the name of Jesus (Ps. 138:2). So, if the word is bread, and it is magnified above the name of Jesus-which is the highest name-then, why would Elimelech and his family leave the house of bread to go to God's "washpot" (Ps. 60:8, 108:9)?

The Lord promises to give the Jew his daily bread (Matt. 6:11). The Lord has provided bread in "the house of bread" again, just as He had in the wilderness journey by manna. So, Naomi rises to leave the world and return to the Lord. The prodigal son came to his senses and realized he had wasted his inheritance in the World and how much better it was at home with the Father and returned to forgiveness, provision, and a feast. The prodigal son was not bitter, but humbled. Naomi is bitter and is returning, defeated, and for carnal reasons.

After dealing with three deaths in her family, her sons marrying heathen, idol-worshiping women, and living with the enemy out of the will of God, the Lord finally reaches her through her belly. Jesus reached the crowds by providing bread to the point that the people tried to force Him to be king, so they could eat for free (John 6:15); because it is all about the flesh. I have read of churches having raffles with money prizes to allure people, so they come for the flesh and not the spirit. I think this is ridiculous, but I understand the appeal to the flesh; they want numbers (quantity) not quality.

I personally accepted Jesus as my Saviour because I did not want to go to hell, the offer appealed to my senses/flesh, I'm not into pain. That's all the theology I understood at the time. I did not want to burn, so with a motive of fear, I surrendered all to the Lord. The belly, fear, valleys, suffering, loss (child, spouse, job, etc.), cancer, foreclosure, ending enmity and having peace, whatever it takes, the Lord will accommodate.

7 Wherefore she went forth out of the place where she was, and her two daughters in law with her; and they went on the way to return unto the land of Judah.

"out of the place where she was" Naomi was in the World in Moab, a bad place, far from God's will for her life. Bad places are like the "far country" and sometimes "the far country" (Luke 15:13) can be just across the street or even in another room in our own house. You do not have to travel far to get away from the Lord and into a bad place. Words, thoughts, and deeds-if not brought under captivity-will lead you astray quickly (2 Cor. 10:5).

Depending on exactly where in Moab Naomi was, what mode of transportation she took back, and whether she took the short cut over the mountains or the long way around, most likely she was only one to three days from home.[22] Naomi suffered so much loss, in so little time, and in such a short distance from the land of praise (Judah). We get into bad places by going there ourselves or by God leading us into the valley Himself. If we go into the valley ourselves, then we can expect chastening from the Lord to get us out and back to where we belong. (Heb. 12:6).

Sometimes, the Lord leads us into the valley to remove an imperfection in our character, to edify us, to strengthen our faith, or to show us something that had never occurred to us before. Sometimes, the Lord leads us in the valley to be of use for someone else that we will meet later in our walk with Christ that we can minister to (2 Cor. 1:4-7).

---

22 Heaton, Paul. Ruth A Story of Devotion, Virtue and Love. Morris Publishing, 2003, p. 8.

Dr. David Jeremiah told a story in the 1990's of how when a member of his congregation would lose a child, he and his wife would go to the hospital to console them as best as they could. Dr. Jeremiah could pray with them, cry with them, and assist them but, could not really comfort them because he had never lost a child; he had not been in that place before. Sometime later, Dr. Jeremiah lost a child. Now, he could comfort someone in the same position (Rom. 8:28), having been in that place himself.[23]

"with her" If you are going to the Lord, why not bring someone with you? cf. Philip, He brings people to the Lord (John 1:45-48; 12:22; Acts 8:37). When you get to heaven, and the Lord looks around and asks you "who you brought to heaven with you", you want to at least have one person to be able to point to. Along those lines, you want to have at least read your bible through one time, at least given one time to the ministry-that was a true sacrifice that really hurt when you gave it-not from your abundance, but from your necessity, been to church one time, and supported at least one missionary, etc.

"return unto the land of Judah" Naomi returns at a different place on the train ride, broken, bitter and beside herself, she leaves the world and returns to the land of praise (Judah). Everyone is on their way somewhere. Ultimately, it is either to heaven or hell!

8 And Naomi said unto her two daughters in law, Go, return each to her mother's house: the LORD deal kindly with you, as ye have dealt with the dead, and with me.

"Go, return each to her mother's house" One has to count the cost to serve the Lord Jesus Christ. Following Jesus will most likely cost you friends (2 Tim. 4:11), family (Matt. 10:34), finances (Luke 14:28; Acts 3:6),

---

23 Jeremiah, David. Turning Point Radio Program, 1995.

and or freedom (Eph. 3:1). Paul counted all these things dung compared to his relationship with Jesus (Phil. 3:7,8,13).

Maybe Naomi-who thus far has been motivated by the material-is having second thoughts about what will become of her daughters-in-law when she arrives home. Maybe she is worried they will not be accepted by her people? Maybe they will be a further embarrassment to her in that not only is she returning bitter and broke, but her children married the enemy and this will be cause for further scorn rather than just leaving to survive the famine? Or maybe she just has the fear of man (Prov. 29:25). Whatever Naomi is thinking though is wrong! How could she leave these two women back in the World to die and go to hell vs. bringing them to the Lord (Ezek. 3:18)? Even if she does not know what will become of them in Bethlehem, one thing is for sure: "Life is short, death for sure, sin the cause, Christ the cure". There is no cure in Moab. Naomi will let them lose their souls to save her from some embarrassment; or them from some persecution (Mark 8:36)!

"the Lord deal kindly with you, as ye have dealt with the dead," In this dispensation of grace, to avoid death and have everlasting life there are a few things that need to be understood. (1.) You can be born once from you mother (physically) and never be born again spiritually and die and go to hell (1st death). Then at the White Throne Judgment (Rev. 20), be cast into the lake of fire (2nd death). So, born once and die twice, or (2.) You can be born once from your mother (physically) and then be born again spiritually (John 3:3) and then not face death at all if you make the Rapture (1 Thess. 4:16-18) or if you die, you simply just go through a door (John 10:9), change your address from wherever you live locally to the third heaven (2 Cor. 12:2) and either way be absent from the body and present with the Lord (2 Cor. 5:8). To achieve option (2.), all you have to know is you're

A.B.C's. ADMIT you are a sinner (Rom. 3:10,23), BELIEVE on the Lord Jesus Christ (Acts 16:31) CONFESS Jesus with your mouth and believe in your heart that God hath raised Jesus from the dead (Rom. 10:9-10).

If you chose option (2.), the Lord will deal **"kindly with you"**: (1.) You are not homeless for all eternity but have a mansion, which for most of us will be an upgrade (John 14:2)! If you do not have a King James Bible, but have a book, such as the N.I.V., you will go to a room-like you have now, not a mansion-so no upgrade! (2.) You will be in a place that surpasses all of your expectations (1 Cor. 2:9) instead of hell. (3.) You will be able to pass through solid objects and travel at the speed of Jesus (Jas. 1:17, 1 John 1:5) which is faster than the speed of light by a few times (John 20:19-26). (4.) You have peace for all eternity in "the land of no mores" (Rev. 21:4); no more death, sorrow, crying, pain, taxes, traffic jams, Monday's, etc. No more lines to use the bathroom either because there is no more blood in your glorified body and no circulatory system, and so once you eat, the food is metabolized immediately, no digestion occurs, thus no restroom lines (Luke 24:39; John 19:34; Heb. 9:12). (5.) We do get to eat in heaven, otherwise it would not be heaven! Jesus ate food in His glorified body after the resurrection (Luke 24:30; John 21:5). There appears to be a buffet as well if you are a glutton (Rev. 19:7,17-18, Ezek. 39:17) or you can reject Jesus and go to hell, where there is no hope, weeping and gnashing of teeth, and eternal torment. Your choice!

If you chose to go to hell, you should consider that: (1.) There is no hope in hell. On earth, we hope for a better job, house, health, lives for our children, and that tomorrow things will get better than today. In hell, there is no hope, no second chances, no reprieve other than appearing at the Great White Throne Judgment just to be cast into the lake of fire, and no changing your mind. Your mind will have been changed from an atheist to a believer once the physical flames "that do not exist", (because you are an atheist), start to burn your metaphysical body (because God has the technology 1 Tim. 6:20), you will have been converted "a day late and a dollar short".

Everyone is a believer eventually; the sinners in hell just believe too late. (2.) Did I mention the flames, there shall be weeping and gnashing of teeth also (Luke 13:28)? (3.) You are alone for all eternity, forgotten by all-even God. Notice there is no mention of the names of Elimelech, Mahlon, or Chilion; just **"the dead"**), and will be reduced to the state of a worm (Mark 9:48) cf. Luke 16 which is the historical account of the rich man and Lazarus, (not a parable). The rich man goes to hell and has no name, but Lazarus, who goes to Abraham's Bosom, retains his name and is known in eternity (1 Cor. 13:12).

Dr. Ruckman states that "a man is composed of a "body," a "soul," and a "spirit" (1 Thess. 5:23). When a man dies in his natural, sinful state, his body decomposes and returns to the dust. (Gen. 3:19). His "spirit" returns to "God who gave it" (Eccl. 12:7, 3:21). But the "soul" is something else. The soul of a man is a spiritual body inside the physical body (Luke 16:23-24). The soul of a lost man is bound for a "second death" (Rev. 20:14), in a place "prepared" for a "serpent" (Matt. 25:41 cf. Rev. 12:9). Christ likened Himself to a "serpent" in His death on the Cross (John 3:14). Moreover, when a lost man dies and goes to hell, Mark 9:44,46 and 48 says, "where the worm dieth not". The Greek word for worm is the word for a red maggot (a maggot being the larva of a fly, as in Beelzebub-the "Lord of flies," another name for the devil [Matt. 12:24]). Psalm 22:6 shows Christ on the cross as "a worm, and no man". The implication of all this is that when a sinner goes to hell he will be just like his "father" (John 8:44) in the same manner that a Christian becomes like His Father when he goes to heaven (1 John 3:1-2); i.e., the sinner "devolves" into a mutant monster that is no longer human (see Rev. 9:1-11). That would explain what Christ meant when he said a man could "lose his own soul" (Mark 8:36), for the soul would lose the bodily shape of the man and become a red maggot. When Christ died on the cross, He not only took sin "**on**" Him (1 Pet. 2:24), He became the complete personification of sin (2 Cor. 5:21). That is the full meaning of the Vicarious (Substitutionary) Atonement: Christ's "**soul**" died as "**an offering**" for your sin (Isa. 53:10)".[24]

9 The LORD grant you that ye may find rest, each *of you* in the house of her husband. Then she kissed them; and they lifted up their voice, and wept.

"that ye may find rest, each of you in the house of her husband." There is no rest outside of Jesus; you must "come unto" Jesus to get rest (Matt. 11:28). You can not have rest without peace. If you KNOW God then you will KNOW peace. If there is NO God then there will be NO peace-(or rest)! Again, Naomi is sending these two women back into the World, to their gods, and wicked way of life so, there will be no rest for them, not even when they die unsaved and go to hell (Rev. 20:10).

Others rests in the bible include: (1.) Creation rest (Heb. 4:3-4). (2.) Millennial rest (Heb. 4:4-8). (3.) Believer's rest (Heb. 4:9-10). (4.) Canaan rest (Heb. 4:6,9).

"Then she kissed them; and they lifted up their voice, and wept." Naomi is giving them "the kiss of death". For Naomi to send Orpah and Ruth back into the World and reject them from having a relationship with God, is an act of betrayal that will lead to the death of their bodies, and subsequently, the torture of their souls eternally. Judas betrayed Jesus with

---

24 (Ruckman Reference Bible 974).

a kiss and this kiss is not much better for Orpah, considering the final outcome (Luke 22:48).

In the scriptures, there is a: (1.) Holy kiss (Rom. 16:16; 1 Cor. 16:20; 2 Cor. 13:12). (2.) Kiss of charity (1 Peter 5:14). (3.) Grieving kiss (Acts 20:37). (4.) Kiss of betrayal (Luke 22:48). (4.) Kiss of deception (Gen. 27:27). (5.) Worshipping kiss (Ps. 2:12).

"wept" Jesus "wept" (John 11:35). Some scholars and preachers say that Jesus wept because of His human side that experienced grief since He was sad that Lazarus was dead. There may be some truth to that statement, but it seems more likely that Jesus wept because the Jews just did not seem to be getting the memo. I mean, if Jesus knew Lazarus was dead (John 11:14) and waited two days until He came, to make sure he was good and dead (John 11:6,39), then he had four days to cry (John 11:39)-Maybe he did; I was not there. But Jesus had told them many times that He was the resurrection (John 11:25), had also proved that He was the Messiah by the miracles that He performed (1 Cor. 1:22) and so the Jews seemed to be slow learners and Jesus groaned in the spirit (John 11:33) more likely because the Jews could not seem to understand who exactly He was due to their lack of faith (Rom. 10:17). So he wept.

There is the exception of Peter, who stated Jesus was the Christ (Matt. 16:16), yet denied Jesus at His arrest vehemently with oaths and cursing (Matt. 26:74). So apparently, he only got the first page of the memo!

There are two kinds of tears that come from sorrow: tears of worldly sorrow and tears of repentance (2 Cor. 7:10). It may be that Orpah is weeping because she knows she will never see Naomi again and Ruth is weeping because she does not want to be left in the World, deserted by Naomi.

Dr. Ruckman states God has a "bottle" for our tears (Ps. 56:8), a "bag" for our transgressions (Job 14:17), and a "book" for our thoughts (Mal.

3:16). With 11,250,00,00,000 tears having been shed since Cain killed Abel (figuring 300 teardrops an ounce), you get enough tears in 6,000 years to float two Lexington-class aircraft carriers.[25]

10 And they said unto her, Surely we will return with thee unto thy people.

"Surely we will return with thee" The daughters-in-law are making a profession. Orpah just professes, while Ruth eventually possesses. Many people profess be a Christian, but a disciple of Christ is altogether a different story. Believing is cheap, costs nothing, and is free. Discipleship is costly and Christ asks us to consider the cost first (Luke 9:58). Christ will work for a believer but discipleship is the result of His work. Believers consider themselves first; Me, Myself, and I (the new Trinity)! Disciples consider Christ first. Believers produce no perfect fruit, but disciples are known by their fruit. Belief saves my soul; an inward act. Discipleship glorifies Christ; an outward act. So, the profession either bears fruit, some thirty, some sixty, some an hundred-fold (Mark 4:20) or it does not bear fruit because it never possessed.

11 And Naomi said, Turn again, my daughters: why will ye go with me? *are* **there yet** *any more* **sons in my womb, that they may be your husbands?**

"are there yet any more sons in my womb, that they may be your husbands?" Naomi is releasing Orpah and Ruth from the law of the kinsmen redeemer (Deut. 25:5), which basically states that if a husband dies, then the Lord would rather the wife marry the husband's brother and keep the inheritance in the family than go to a stranger. The problem is that Naomi has no more sons to offer for marriage and seems to think that

---

25 (Ruckman Reference Bible 807).

it is more important for these young women to go back into the World, remarry, and live after the flesh, than to come to Bethlehem, "the house of bread", and have ever lasting life (Rom. 8:1-2). Naomi is thinking temporarily rather than eternally-as usual-because her heart and treasure is in the World (Matt. 6:19).

12 Turn again, my daughters, *go your way*; for I am too old to have an husband. If I should say, I have hope, *if* I should have an husband also to night, and should also bear sons;

"**I am too old to have a husband**" If the Lord could provide a child for Abram and Sarai when she was barren and past the age to bear children (Gen. 17:16), He surely could produce a husband for Naomi from His warehouse (Matt. 19:26). I believe a husband is easier to supply than an elderly, barren woman having a child.

There are several miraculous births in the Bible where the Lord provided a child against the odds that include: (1.) Sarai (Gen. 17:16). (2.) Hanna (1 Sam.1:20). (3.) Rachel (Gen. 30:24) (4.) Manoah's wife (Judg.13:3). (5.) Rebecca (Gen. 25:21). (6.) Elizabeth (Luke 1:13) (7.) The Shunamite woman (2 Kings 4:17). (8.) Mary (Luke 1:31). The Lord gathered the waters in the Red Sea to part with just a blast from His nostrils (Exod. 15:8) and gave all these women children miraculously, so not a problem at all to find a husband!

13 Would ye tarry for them till they were grown? would ye stay for them from having husbands? nay, my daughters; for it grieveth me much for your sakes that the hand of the LORD is gone out against me.

"**Would ye tarry**" Jesus told the disciples to tarry ye here and watch with me (Matt. 26:38). There are the FEW disciples-twelve (John 6:70).

There are the CALLED, which are three- Peter, James and John (Matt. 17:1). There is the CHOSEN: John (John 13:23).

While the world is tarrying at the wine (Prov. 23:30), a Christian should be tarrying in prayer (Matt. 26:38). Jesus brings us to a point in our life where we can go no further, so He leaves us at the gate (Matt. 26:36). The question is "can you go a little further"? (Matt. 26:39). A disciple has to tarry to grow in Jesus spiritually, and then go (further).

There are seven stages of Christian growth: (1.) "Babes" (1 Cor. 3:1). (2.) "Little children" (1 John 2:1). (3.) "Children" (Gal. 3:26). (4.) "Young men" (1 John 2:13). (5.) "Fathers" (1 John 2:13). (6.) "Elders" (1 Pet. 5:1). (7.) "Aged" (Phile. 9).

There is your will for your life, and then there is God's will for your life. Where the two meet is at a place called the Cross and someone has to die! "For if there be first a willing mind, it is accepted according to that a man hath, and not according to that he hath not" (2 Cor. 8:12). God looks on the heart (1 Sam. 16:7) to see if we are willing to tarry and then obey. This is a key verse to finding the will of God in your life.

You will not find the will of God for your life in a simple "bless me, Lord" prayer. To find the will of God for your life requires many trips to the altar (Gen. 15:8-10). Abraham, at approximately eighty years old, had to go and collect the animals to be offered, which takes time. Abraham then had to divide and dress the animals which takes even more time for an elderly man. Abraham had to offer the best of his animals in their prime (three years old) of their production and value to satisfy the Lord. Then, upon offering the sacrifice, to know God's will for his life, the fowls (Satan) came down upon the carcasses and Abraham had to drive them away, which is even more work for an old man. The point is that Abraham had to make many trips to the altar, the sacrifices were costly, and it took some time to understand God's will for his life. God tests a Christian, and here Orpah and Ruth, on what they are willing to do. The response to that test determines the course for the rest of their life.

The tests run like this: "Could I take your baby, your wife, or your husband"? "Would you spend the rest of your life in a wheelchair for me if I wanted you to"? "Would you be willing to die a slow death for me"? "Would you be willing to go to Africa as a missionary or lay down your life in Iraq"? [26]

Orpah does not want to tarry and goes back, settling for second best for her life, while Ruth tarries and receives *exceeding abundantly* above all that we ask or think, according to the power that worketh in us (Eph. 3:20) from the Lord.

"the hand of the Lord is gone out against me" "Choose ye whom ye will serve today" (Josh. 24:15) and let the chips fall where they may. It is not the Lord's will for any to perish (2 Pet. 3:9) and the Lord will go to great lengths to get our attention to keep that from happening but this is not Burger King and so you can not have it your way! It is going to be the Lord's way; the easy way or the hard way, but it will be His way! Cf. Jonah going the hard way to Nineveh (Jon. 1:17), Baalim going the hard way to get a dollar (Num. 22:27), the one hit wonder preacher that died the hard way (1 Kings 13), Agrippa giving God the glory the hard way (Acts 12:23) and even Paul going to Rome the hard way via getting arrested in Jerusalem (Acts. 21:33). ***Note to self, if you go against the Lord, expect turbulence!

Oswald Chambers says "When God brings the blank space, see that you do not fill it in, but wait. The blank space may come in order to teach you what sanctification means, or it may come after sanctification to teach you what service means".[27] Many a Christian would do good to tarry on the Lord, thus saving a life frustration by going it alone.

---

26 (Ruckman Reference Bible 1539).
27 Chambers, Oswald. My Utmost for His Highest. Barbour and Company, Inc. 1935, Jan 4.

14 And they lifted up their voice, and wept again: and Orpah kissed her mother in law; but Ruth clave unto her.

"Orpah kissed her mother in law; but Ruth clave unto her" Three were WASHED UP: Elimelech, Mahlon, and Chilion (death). Naomi gets WASHED (chastened), Orpah is being WASHED OUT (of salvation), while Ruth is being WASHED IN (salvation)![28]

Orpah has seen better days, but it is time to go back to the farm and start all over and hope for the best, keep smiling, and keep a stiff upper-lip. "I can do all things through Christ which strengtheneth me" (Phil. 4:13), which means in English, you can not do anything without Christ. So, Orpah will be on her own again, in the World, comfortable in her sin and serving her false gods.

Ruth is separating from the world, sanctifying herself, supporting the elderly-true religion (Jas. 1:27), and going to receive a great inheritance. No doubt Ruth has had a taste of this Jewish God from her husband and in-laws Elimelech and Naomi. No doubt Ruth knew what God did to the Egyptians-as most of the world at that time knew-and just can not bear to go back into the world after having been enlightened (Heb. 6:4). And so she cleaves to her ticket (Naomi) to find salvation among the Jews.

15 And she said, Behold, thy sister in law is gone back unto her people, and unto her gods: return thou after thy sister in law.

"her people, and her gods" Orpah has gone back to her ways, seeing no prospect for a husband in Bethlehem. Bob Jones Sr. said "never sacrifice the permanent on the altar of the immediate". Orpah is seeking Mr. Right now, not Mr. Right. Orpah's gods, Molech and Chemosh, would not be able to supply her needs (Isaiah 44:17). "And the residue thereof he maketh

---

28 (Ruckman Reference Bible 416).

a god, *even* his graven image: he falleth down unto it, and worshippeth *it*, and prayeth unto it, and saith, Deliver me; for thou *art* my god." But the god can not supply or deliver cf. (Phil. 4:13).

"return" Naomi has told her daughter-in-laws three times to return and Orpah has gone; Ruth is told for the fourth time here. Peter denied Jesus three times (Matt. 26:34) and had to affirm Him three times on the seashore (John 21:17). Jesus prayed three times in Gethsemane to let the cup pass from Him (Matt. 26:44) and the apostle Paul prayed three times to have his thorn in his flesh removed (2 Cor. 12:8). The World, where Orpah has gone, says "three's a charm"!

Orpah has taken the worldly counsel of Naomi and returned to the world. The angel, after the resurrection, said "tell His disciples and Peter" (Mark 16:7). "And Peter", because Peter had lost his discipleship for not following Jesus, but not his salvation (Luke 22:32). Orpah is no longer in the family; she has lost her place along with her inheritance, her salvation, and a relationship with God.

Orpah seems to make this decision prejudiced by her flesh to find a husband who can support her because her gods in Moab surely can not (Jeremiah 2:28), and she is not willing to trust the God of the Hebrews. We make our decisions based on what we love or what is first in our heart. If God is first, we will seek His perfect will for our life. If not whatever your god is will determine the outcome of the path you take. Rather than tarry for God's will in her life, Orpah seeks the god of her heart-a husband so she can survive. Ruth is following Naomi looking for God, not a husband!

16 And Ruth said, Intreat me not to leave thee, *or* to return from following after thee: for whither thou goest, I will go; and where thou lodgest, I will lodge: thy people *shall be* my people, and thy God my God:

"for whither thou goest, I will go; and where thou lodgest, I will lodge" Many times a person will launch out into an endeavor based on emotion rather than a sure calling from the Lord and failure occurs because Christ "was not in it". To have a burden for something, does not necessarily translate into a calling from the Lord to minister to that burden. There are only so many hours in a day and so many dollars in a budget, a Christian can not save the world singlehandedly and champion every worthy cause, so we have to seek the Lord's will in a matter.

We all have a specific job to do in the body of Christ and the eyes ca not be trying to do the hand's job (1 Cor. 12:21). A Christian cannot be obligated to participate by a feeling, pressure, or what the majority is doing; but has to rely on the guidance of the Lord alone.

In the gospels there was a man, who probably was sincere, who wanted to follow the Lord. The man said he would follow **whithersoever** Jesus went without counting the cost. When Jesus told him "The foxes have holes, and the birds of the air have nests **(lodging)**, but the Son of Man hath nowhere to lay His head" (Matt. 8:20), the man apparently was no longer interested; as there is no account of him following Jesus.

Ruth is a possessor, not a professor because she cleaves to Naomi and follows Naomi to her people and to her God. In Exod. 12:3-5, the Bible speaks of "a lamb" in (vs.3), "the lamb" in (vs.4), and "your lamb' in (vs.5). Spiritually speaking, Ruth is going to meet "a lamb" versus indulging in another pagan ritual that accomplishes nothing like Orpah has returned to. Ruth is going to meet "the lamb" not another false god like Molech or Chemosh who cannot help her or Orpah's situation. Ruth is going to make the lamb "her lamb" and gain eternal life. You can know that Jesus was "A" lamb, and He was "THE" lamb, but if you do not make Him "YOUR" lamb, you will die and go to hell (Jas. 2:19)! Orpah, as the rich young ruler (Matt. 19), turned herself away from a blessing because of the hardness of her heart (Matt. 19:8), the desires of her heart for a husband (Jer. 17:9), and because of her lack of faith (Matt. 17:20).

17 Where thou diest, will I die, and there will I be buried: the LORD do so to me, and more also, *if ought* **but death part thee and me.**

    "death part thee and me." Vs. 16-17 are recited as wedding vows in many marriages. The King James Bible is spoken by saved and unsaved people every day, in every generation unbeknownst to many of them. We speak the Elizabethan English language automatically! "You will never get rid of this book!" (Dr. Ruckman). Some examples of modern sayings used from the Bible include: 2 Chron. 9:4 "took my breath away", 2 Chron. 9:6 "seeing is believing". Judg. 8:16 "taught them" (modern vernacular-you got schooled). Further the K.J.V. Elizabethan English is how people still speak today, not in the "modern more up to date" versions. Cf.

    K.J.V. vs. N.I.V. "MODERN" language used today:

1. Gen. 30:27 "learned by experience" vs. "learned by divination".
2. Gen. 31:37 "searched all my stuff" vs. "searched all my goods".
3. 2 Chron. 36:3 "king of Egypt put him down" vs. "dethroned him".
4. Neh. 13:11 "put him in his place" vs. "stationed them at their posts".
5. Prov. 4:25 "let thine eyes look right on" vs. "fix your gaze".
6. Isa. 65:5 "holier than thou" vs. "too sacred for you".[29]

    In all of these examples listed, the KJV reading is easier to understand and more similar to how we still speak English in 2018 as opposed

---

29 Gipp, Sam. jesus-is-savior.com/Bible/1611_authorized_king_james.htm.

to the other versions that the reading makes no sense, nor is it written in today's vernacular! Further the new Bible never update the word "dung" (Phil. 3:8), why not?

The world revolves around England, not Rome or Alexandria, Egypt. English is the universal language spoken today. Absolute time is calculated in Greenwich, England. Absolute temperature is measured in English (British Thermal Unit-BTU), Absolute location is located in Greenwich, England; longitude and latitude are measured from the equator and Greenwich, England. Absolute truth is in the K.J.V. not any book from Rome or Egypt.

"the LORD do so to me, and more also" This quote is used in the O.T. by people making an oath or a curse. Cf. (1.) Here (Ruth) 1:17, (2.) Ben-hadad (2 Kings 6:31), (3.) Samuel (1 Sam. 3:17), (4.) David (1 Sam. 25:22).

18 When she saw that she was stedfastly minded to go with her, then she left speaking unto her.

"stedfastly minded" Ruth was not double minded (Jas. 1:8); she is not wavering at all in her commitment (Jas. 1:6). Jesus said "No man, having put his hand to the plow and looking back, is fit for the Kingdom of God" (Luke 9:62). Jesus "stedfastly" set His face to go to Jerusalem (Luke 9:51) and went. The apostles continued "stedfastly" in doctrine and fellowship (Acts 2:42). As the martyr Steven was being stoned to death, he looked stedfastly into heaven, and saw the glory of God (Acts 7:56). As Christians, we need to make up our mind about following Jesus and remain stedfast, nothing wavering, nothing competing with our Lord, and having our eyes focused on Him as Steven did.

19 So they two went until they came to Bethlehem. And it came to pass, when they were come to Bethlehem, that all the city was moved about them, and they said, *Is* this Naomi?

"went until they came to Bethlehem." Ruth went all the way, she did not quit, she did not turn back. In the parable of the sower (Matt. 13), three fourths of the people that heard the word of the Lord quit, went back, or never even started.

The greatest preacher that ever preached, Jesus, was only able to bring fruit from twenty five percent of the audience (Matt. 13). Further, after three and-a-half years of preaching, miracles, and even rising from the dead, Jesus left a church of one hundred and twenty followers in an upper room (Acts 1:15).

Ruth had ears to her hear (Mat. 11:15) and was one of the twenty five percent. We have to go all the way down on our knees (accepting Jesus), if we want to go all the way up to heaven by salvation. Paul says that each one of us has a race to run (Heb. 12:1) and that we will not be crowned if we do not finish our course (2 Tim. 4:7) and that we have to strive lawfully to be crowned (2 Tim. 2:5). Ruth's eye was single (Matt. 6:22); she was determined and by the grace of God she made it.

However, many do not make it. James Knox, in a sermon given in 2012, stated according to the 1991 Britannica Book of the year, that the total population of the world is 5 billion, 292 million. There are 935 million Muslims, non-religious make up 866 million, Hindus 705 million, Buddhists 303 million, Atheists 233 million, Chinese folk religions 180 million, New Religionists 138 million, Tribal 92 million, Sikhs 18 million, Jews 17 million, Shamanists 10 million, Confusions 5.8 million, Bahai-5.3 million, Jaians-3.6 million, Shintoists 3.1 million, other religions 17,930,000.

Further, 3 billion 523 million 430,000 are excluded from the way the truth and the life and Rapture. 995 million 780,000 are Roman Catholics (do not believe they have to be born again). 363 million 290,000 Protestant, Orthodox 166 million 942,000, Anglican 72 million 980,000, 160 million and other Christians includes cults. For every 1,000, 300 are Christian in word only, 300 trusting water baptism for salvation, 300 counting on good works to save them, 50 are workers of iniquity seeking to ruin the Churches social, political, and moral objectives, 40 know the way to eternal life but have not taken it yet, so there are less than 1 million trusting Jesus only. Jesus was not kidding about the narrow road and your yard in Heaven just got bigger because not many make it!!![30]

"Is this Naomi?" Naomi has changed, the world has worn her down to where she is almost unrecognizable, she is full of bitterness and shame. Naomi has been gone for ten years and finds herself in the same condition as the prodigal son having to return home broke, beaten down physically, and busted up emotionally. The way of the transgressor is hard (Prov. 13:5). Sin makes us unrecognizable. How many stories could each of us tell of someone in our lives that we knew that seemed to have "the world by its horns" just to run across them some years down the road and they are worn down, haggard and barely recognizable because of the sinful choices they made?

Lucifer was originally an anointed cherub that covered the throne of God (Ezek. 28:14). He sealest up the sum, full of wisdom, and was perfect in beauty (Ezek. 28:12). Lucifer was a creature composed of organic and inorganic material. God made Lucifer with every precious stone and completed him with tabrets and pipes (wind and stringed instruments); there was none created to his likening.

However, Lucifer fell from this glorious position because of his rebellion caused by his pride and his name was changed to Satan (Isa. 14:16). Lucifer because of sin had become unrecognizable compared

---

30 Knox, James. Sermon, 2012.

to what He once was in God's creation (Job 41). After the fall, Lucifer became a red dragon (Rev. 12:3), appeared on earth as a roaring lion (1 Pet. 5:8) and as an angel of light (2 Cor. 11:14). Thus, Satan has four appearances in the Bible; starting as a cherub and ending as a man in the sides of the pit (Isa. 14). Cf. Jesus appears through five manifestations in the Bible: (1.) As the Angel of lord (Acts 27; Gal. 4), (2.) As son of man seated at the right hand of God in third heaven, (3.) In us, if we are saved, in the person of the Holy Spirit (Col. 1:27), (4.) The Lamb slain before the foundation of the world (Rev. 13:8), and (5.) As the lion of the tribe of Judah (Rev. 5:5).

Jesus pictures the ultimate damage that sin can inflict upon a person "As many were astonied at thee; His visage was so marred more than any man, and His form more than the sons of men" (Isa. 52:14). Jesus went from being the rose of Sharon, and the Lillie of the valleys, to becoming sin for us (2 Cor. 5:21), and so identified with sin, that the Father had to turn His back His own son (Matt. 27:46). cf. Jesus will never turn His back on a believer (Heb. 13:5-6).

20 And she said unto them, Call me not Naomi, call me Mara: for the Almighty hath dealt very bitterly with me.

"For the almighty hath dealt very bitterly with me" Naomi accuses God where as "Job in all this did not sin with his lips nor charge God foolishly" (Job 1:22). Maybe God has chastened Naomi bitterly. Maybe the wages of sin has dealt bitterly with her (Rom. 6:23)? Many times, we blame God for the results that occur from the poor decisions we make and thus, experience the cause and effect of our actions.

The success prosperity doctrine-that is widely preached today-would never consider that God would deal bitterly with one of His children.

Propagators of this heresy would say "as a child of God, you should not suffer, all your needs should be met, you should just name and claim (blab and grab) it, your best destiny, life, and the best you are right here and right now"! It would never occur one time to such false preachers that God is not some big teddy-bear up in heaven who understands your sin, is okay with it, and does not judge you as long as you do the best you can. At the gym, you get out what you put in. There is no minimum input and maximum output, but more like the law of diminishing returns which rewards you accordingly. Naomi reaped what she sowed (Gal. 6:7-9).

21 I went out full, and the LORD hath brought me home again empty: why *then* call ye me Naomi, seeing the LORD hath testified against me, and the Almighty hath afflicted me?

"testified against me" Naomi seems to not see her part in any thing that has transpired for the last ten years. To be honest, I do not know when the last time was when I had a car problem that made me late to work, that I got on my knees and proclaimed to God how good He was, and what a blessing to have a dead battery, but other better Christians in the Bible had such responses.

If we would judge ourselves better than Naomi did, then God would not have to judge and testify against us (1 Cor. 11:31). Naomi is still carnal, blaming, ungrateful and just not getting that she has gotten exactly what she deserves. Naomi has made no spiritual growth whatsoever.

No matter what David did, he always took the blame, admitted he was wrong, repented, and made things right with the Lord and those around him. David had a great attitude and response, unlike Naomi.

Paul went so far as to say the he GLORIED in his infirmities and that he took PLEASURE in reproaches, in necessities, in persecutions, in distresses (2 Cor. 12:5,10). I have not made it to that level of a disciple yet and neither has Naomi!

22 So Naomi returned, and Ruth the Moabitess, her daughter in law, with her, which returned out of the country of Moab: and they came to Bethlehem in the beginning of barley harvest.

"barley harvest" Dr. Ruckman states, the beginning of the barley harvest is from late March in the lowlands to early May in higher elevations. The reason this time period is mentioned is that Naomi and Ruth came back to Bethlehem "flat broke". They had no money, no job, and no food.[31] Things were bleak, to say the least. What appears to be a problem will become a profitable outcome, because the Lord can furnish a table in the wilderness (Ps. 78:19) and His arm is not too short that it cannot save (Isa. 59:1) in the city!

Notice the providence of God's timing for them to return at a time of financial opportunity. Preachers say, "God is never late, rarely comes early, but is always on time"! cf. Joseph in prison (Gen. 40-41). Joseph had correctly interpreted the dreams of the baker and steward while they were in ward and asked the steward not to forget him when he returned to his position serving Pharaoh. However, the steward returned to work and forgot all about Joseph, until a full two years later (God's providence; God did not forget) when Pharaoh had some bad dreams. The steward then remembered that Joseph had correctly interpreted his dreams and referred Pharaoh to Joseph to provide relief. If the steward would have told Pharaoh about this young Jewish man in jail and his ability to interpret dreams upon his release two years earlier, then Pharaoh could have cared less as he had no need for Joseph's services and the opportunity

---

31 (Ruckman Ruth Commentary 378).

would have passed to no avail. However, God's providence brought Joseph into Pharaoh's sights at precisely the right time to be of service (minister to) to Pharaoh, thus promoting Joseph at the right time for his problem to be turned into a profitable experience. Remember, our promotions always come from God who is the North at the precise, right time (Ps. 75:7).

CHAPTER TWO

RUTH GOES TO WORK

2:1 And Naomi had a kinsman of her husband's, a mighty man of wealth, of the family of Elimelech; and his name *was* Boaz.

"a kinsman of her husband's" Here in chapter two, a beautiful example of redemption for the Christian is revealed in the kinsman redeemer of Boaz, who is a type of Jesus. As previously stated (according to the law Deut. 25:5), now that Ruth is a widow, Boaz has an obligation to marry Ruth and perform the duty of a husband's brother unto her. God is working behind the scenes here (Rom. 8:28), providentially to reward Ruth for leaving the world and seeking a relationship with Him. Knowing that Ruth is destitute, the Lord will show us in the next chapters doors opening for her, favor being obtained, and all of her needs being met "exceeding abundantly" above all that she ever expected (Eph. 3:20) via God's providence.

Just as Ruth needed Boaz to redeem her by buying her back out of the World and placing her in the family of Elimelech again, we as sinners needed a redeemer as well to buy us back from the wages of sin (Rom. 6:23).

The Bible says that "all have sinned and come short of the glory of God" (Rom. 3:10, 23). As sinners sold to sin, a payment (ransom/propitiation) had to be made to satisfy God's holiness and judgment on sin. God is an eternal being and when we sin, we have to pay for that sin eternally. It was not possible for the blood of bulls and goats to pay for our sins, as offered in the O.T., so Jesus had to die on the cross (Heb. 9:12-14) and shed His perfect, eternal blood to redeem us back to the Father. Jesus is our near kinsman redeemer who paid our ransom and proclaimed on the cross that "it is finished" (John 19:30), referring to completing the redemption process.

When we were born, we were born in Adam's image; not God's, as commonly misunderstood by people ignorant of Bible doctrine. Adam was created in God's image (Gen. 1:27), but since Adam fell through sin, now all people are created in Adam's image and not Gods. To regain God's image (John 1:12), we have to be born again spiritually (John 3).

There is a great story told of redemption that is about a boy and his sailboat. It seems this boy bought the materials, spent the time, and made a sailboat. The boy spared no expense and fearfully and wonderfully (Ps. 139:14) created the sailboat with the utmost care. He took the sailboat out to play with it and somehow it became lost. Later, the boy was walking down the street and saw his sailboat in the window of a store. The little boy went in and told the shop keeper that that was his sailboat and it had gotten lost and that he wanted it back. The shop keeper told the boy that now it was his sailboat and if he wanted it back, he would have to buy it from him. The boy then went to work, saved up the money, and returned to the store and bought the sail boat back. Upon leaving the story, the boy exclaimed "Now you're mine twice. I made you the first time and you were mine. Then I lost you and I bought you back"! As the boy made and bought back the lost sailboat, so God made us, lost us to sin, and has bought us back through His son's vicarious death on the cross, making atonement and redemption now possible.

"a mighty man of wealth" A noticeable contrast appears between Elimelech and Boaz. While Elimelech left the "house of bread" (Bethlehem) and praising God (Judah) to run to the world (Moab; God's "washpot") to meet his needs and loses everything including his life, Boaz waits on the Lord and survives the famine becoming **"a mighty man of wealth"**. "There is nothing wrong with obtaining wealth and possessions as long as the possessions do not possess you". Jesus said in Luke 9:24 "For whosoever will save his life shall lose it: but whosoever will lose his life for my sake, the same shall save it". Elimelech died trying to save his flesh and gain possessions, but Boaz's life has been spared and made wealthy because of trusting the Lord.

The foolish virgins of Matt. 25 are another example of contrast between riding out the storm with the Lord, as opposed to settling for the worlds temporary comfort (crumbs) at an eternal price. The foolish virgins who were in the World and not caring for the things of the Lord, were not allowed entry into the wedding when the time came. They lost all that they had and since they did not have the oil, even that was taken away which they had (Matt. 13:12). The wise virgins that did not leave off caring, for the things of the Lord, and who were prepared, gained entrance to the wedding without delay. The wise virgins gained eternal reward (wealth) that cannot be corrupted here on earth (Matt. 6:19).

Finally, there is the story of Abraham and Lot. While Lot selfishly chose the better land, instead of yielding to his elder Abraham, he pitched his tent toward Sodom. Lot eventually went from looking into the World (Sodom), to making business or necessity trips into the World, to living permanently in the World. Consequently, Lot lost all that he had and escaped the World with only his two daughters (2 Cor. 6:14). "One man's trash is another man's treasure!" So, Abraham took the second-choice land, that Lot did not want, and ended up gaining the whole world, (Rom. 4:13) becoming "**a mighty man of wealth**".

In the Bible, satan is also said to be "a mighty man". According to Job 22:8, "the mighty man" (Satan) Bible had the earth; and the honourable man (Adam) dwelt in it. Satan is mighty because he once held the position of being the fifth cherub that covereth the throne of God (Lucifer), before being cast down (Isa. 14) to the sides of the pit. Adam is said to be the honourable man because he gave his life for his wife (Eve), as Christ gave His life for the Church (1 John 3:16; Eph. 5:25).

Finally, Jesus is "a mighty man". "For ye know the grace of our Lord Jesus Christ, that, though He was rich, yet for your sakes He became poor, that ye through His poverty might be rich" (2 Cor. 8:9). According to Matt. 12:29, "the mighty man" (Jesus) bound the strong man's (Satan) house and spoiled it. "And having spoiled principalities and powers, He made a shew of them openly, triumphing over them in it" (Col. 2:15).

"**Boaz**" The name "Boaz" has several meanings, according to varied sources. "In him is strength"[32] seems to be a good fit for his reputation and moral character. With one of the definitions of Boaz meaning "strength", it is important to remember that "For when we were yet without strength, in due time Christ died for the ungodly" (Rom. 5:6-11); the Lord is our strength (Ps. 46:1). The name Boaz also appears in 1 Chron. 3:17, as one of the names of the entrance pillars of Solomon's temple, the other being Jachin (established). The idea being the Lord's house is established in strength.[33]

---

32 en.wikipedia.org/wiki/Boaz.
33 (Ruckman Ruth Commentary 356).

2 And Ruth the Moabitess said unto Naomi, Let me now go to the field, and glean ears of corn after *him* in whose sight I shall find grace. And she said unto her, Go, my daughter.

"Let me now go to the field" Ruth and Naomi have needs that they cannot supply, being widows. They are broke financially, but Ruth has prepared her heart to humble herself and work. "But He giveth more grace. Wherefore He saith, God resisteth the proud, but giveth grace unto the humble" (Jas. 4:6). If you submit to the Lord (Jas. 4:7), cast all your cares upon Him (1 Pt 5:7), and flee from Satan, the Lord will provide (Phil. 4:19)!

Ruth is not looking for a handout, food stamps, welfare, an easy way out, or for the Church to take care of her (1 Tim. 5:3,11,16); Ruth is looking for work! Ruth understood the biblical principle that if any would not work, neither should he eat (2 Thess. 3:10).

"find grace" Grace (G.R.A.C.E.): God's Riches At Christ's Expense (unmerited favor). Ruth needs grace (Rom. 5:2). She is a Moabitess, stranger, enemy to Israel and God. She is in a hopeless situation seeking favor with God and Naomi's people. Ruth has nothing to fall back on now to survive; she is without strength (Rom. 5). Even though she is a Gentile, stranger, sinner, deserving nothing, she is hoping against all hope that God-knowing her heart-will move and provide for her cf. Heb. 4:16 "Let us therefore come boldly unto the throne of grace, that we may obtain mercy, and find grace to help in time of need".

Ruth, like Mephibosheth (2 Sam. 9), has nothing at all to offer to anyone. She brings no benefit to the table and has no value (her being a Gentile widow and Mephibosheth a handicapped man). Both come from the World (Moab and Lo-debar) hiding from, or ignorant of God. Both probably suffered from low self-esteem due to their circumstances and both are excellent candidates for God's grace, as they have nowhere else to turn but to the Lord (Isa. 55).

3 And she went, and came, and gleaned in the field after the reapers: and her hap was to light on a part of the field *belonging* unto Boaz, who *was* of the kindred of Elimelech.

"**after the reapers**" Ruth is taking advantage of God's welfare system. If a Jew did not have money to buy food, he was allowed to go into another man's field during the harvest and pick up the grain left on the ground from the main harvest. Lev. 19:9-10 commanded the Jewish landowner to leave the corners of the fields for the poor to glean. The Lord provides down to the last scruple!

Concerning the harvest, there are three stages of reaping: (1.) The "first fruits", (2.) The "main harvest", and (3.) The "gleanings". As in farming, this formula applies to the resurrection of the dead also (1 Cor. 15). (1.) Christ was the first fruits of them that "slept" (vs. 20). (2.) They that are Christ's at His coming (1 Thess. 4:16-18) are the main harvest (vs. 23). (3.) Finally, cometh the end, the post tribulation saints that are raptured out of the tribulation just before the second advent (vs.24).

Jesus's disciples plucked corn on the Sabbath from another man's field and were allowed to eat without trespassing or committing theft (Luke 6:1). The Lord's "welfare system" provides even for the sparrows of the air (Matt. 6:26). If the Lord will take the time to clothe the grass of the field better than king Solomon, which today is and tomorrow is cast into the oven, then He will provide work and food for his children.

"**her hap was to light on a part of the field belonging unto Boaz**" Cha Ching! 777 or all pineapples; Ruth has won the lottery! "Our hap is God's map"! Hap means happenstance. God's providence is being demonstrated again as Ruth just happens-out of all the fields in Bethlehem-to pick the one field owned by a single, wealthy, humble, family member of excellent character that will become her husband (Rom. 8:28) a.k.a. "The most eligible Bachelor". Oswald Chambers says "The disciple who abides in Jesus *is* the will of God, and his apparently free choices are God's foreordained decrees. Mysterious? Logically contradictory and absurd? Yes, but a glorious truth to a saint".[34] Ruth picked the right field, although the Lord led her to it.

4 And, behold, Boaz came from Bethlehem, and said unto the reapers, The LORD *be* with you. And they answered him, The LORD bless thee.

"**The LORD be with you**" Boaz is a humble man who realizes that every good and perfect gift comes from above (Jas. 1:17) and is thankful for them. Nothing is outside of the egis or attention of God. Everything a person ever does is completely dependent upon the blessing of God, especially farming! Your very breath is in the hands of the Lord (Dan. 5:23). No one can stay God's hand (Dan. 4:35). You can do all things through Christ. So if the Lord is not blessing what you do, it will come to naught (Phil. 4:13).

"**The LORD**" is the name of the Father (Jude 5), the Son (Phil. 2:11), and the Holy Ghost (2 Cor. 3:17). The transliteration of the name "Jehovah" is represented in the Bible by the word LORD. Jehovah means: Je-"open arms", Ho-"window", Vah "nail". Jehovah means God reached out of heaven with outstretched arms and put a nail in His son's hands to save sinners (Zech.10:4; Ezra 9:8). The name Jehovah appears seven times in the King James version, seven being the number of completion or perfection: (1). Exod. 6:3, (2). Ps. 83:18, (3). Isa. 12:2, (4). Isa. 26:4, (5). Gen. 22:14, (6). Exod. 17:15, (7). Judges 6:24.

The name of the LORD was not known in the O.T. cf. Manoah asked the name of the angel of the LORD and was told "it was a secret" (Judges 13:18). But in (vs. 19), the angel does "wondrously" and Jesus

---

34 (Chambers June 7).

name shall be called wonderful (Isa. 9:6). Jacob asks the name of the Lord (Gen. 32:29). In (vs. 30) Jacob states that he has seen God, face to face. In 1 John 1:1, the Bible says "which we have seen with our eyes, which we have looked upon, and our hands have handled", Jacob handled God in a wrestling match, face to face! Prov. 30:4 asks "Who hath ascended up into heaven or descended? who hath gathered the wind in His fists? who hath bound the waters in a garment? who hath established all the ends of the earth? what is His name, and what is His son's name, if thou canst tell"; the answer is in (vs. 5) "Every word of God is pure". The word of God is the title of Jesus Christ (Rev. 19:13; 1 John 5:7; John 1:1,14).[35]

Dr. Ruckman says "For some reason, the King James translators took it upon themselves to capitalize seven words in Exodus chapter 3: "I AM THAT I AM, I AM." If you add this to the second revelation of the name given in Exodus 6:3, you have a sentence that says: I AM THAT I AM; I AM JEHOVAH." Strangely enough, the last set of capitals shows up in Rev. 19:16, where a full sentence would say "I AM THAT I AM; I AM JEHOVAH, KING OF KINGS, AND LORD OF LORDS".[36]

5 Then said Boaz unto his servant that was set over the reapers, Whose damsel *is* this?

"Whose damsel is this" The word damsel appears numerous times in the Bible, see any concordance. Webster's 1828 dictionary defines damsel as: "*noun* A young woman. Formerly, a young man or woman of noble or genteel extraction; as *damsel* Pepin; *damsel* Richard, prince of Wales. It is now used only of young women and is applied to any class of young unmarried women, unless to the most vulgar, and sometimes to country girls".[37]

---

35 (Ruckman Reference Bible 894).
36 (Ruckman Reference Bible 104).
37 (Webster Dictionary).

Ruth has caught Boaz's attention, most likely because she looks and is dressed differently from the other Jewish people there gleaning. Ruth, a Moabite, is of Egyptian descent which is Hamitic in origin (Gen. 12); therefore, her skin tone would stand darker when compared with a Jew.

Devotionally speaking, a Christian (saved disciple) should stand out from the unsaved world. A Christian should be able to point out to lost people that God's last name is not "damn". A Christian should have no desire to stand around while on break telling "off color" jokes with his peers. A Christian should have so much evidence of being a disciple of Christ, that if they were to go on trial in a court of law for being a Christian, they should be found guilty immediately by the jury. There should be no questions at a Christian's funeral as to whether or not the deceased was saved or not. A Christian should stand out!

6 And the servant that was set over the reapers answered and said, It *is* the Moabitish damsel that came back with Naomi out of the country of Moab:

"the servant that was set over the reapers answered and said, It is the Moabitish damsel" Notice that Ruth's name is not given. Devotionally, this is because our name is not important compared with our Saviour's. The important thing that matters most is; did we bring glory and honor to the Lord Jesus Christ (Rev. 4:11)? The servant set over the reapers did not know Ruth's name but he knew the manner of her work (Acts 4:7,12, Col. 3:17).

Dr. Greg Estep states "this servant is over the reapers, a picture of the Holy Ghost, God of the harvest, calling out a bride for his master. No name given as he is to magnify his master" (John 16:14).[38] Ruth pictures the Church age. Ruth is in the field (the World) harvesting and gathering, as we should be doing as well until the Lord comes!

---

38 (Estep Ruth Class).

Further no name is given to the widow that gave all her earnings (her two cents) (Mark 12:42), to the young lad who supplied five barley loaves and two fish (John 6:9) that the Lord used to feed the crowd, or even to the little maid that waited on Naaman's wife who suggested that Naaman go to Israel for the healing of his leprosy (2 Kings 5:3), but their actions are recorded forever in the Bible and they are known in heaven cf. names like Frank Sinatra, Elvis Presley, Nelson Rockefeller, George Bush, Bill Clinton, Mic Jagger and any other celebrity star, sports figure, politician, etc. whose names will be forgotten for all eternity (Rev 20).

7 And she said, I pray you, let me glean and gather after the reapers among the sheaves: so she came, and hath continued even from the morning until now, that she tarried a little in the house.

"**so she came, and hath continued even from the morning until now**" Ruth's work ethic reveals that she is loyal. Ruth, as Orpah, could have taken the easy way out and stayed in her country and left Naomi to her own circumstances. However, Ruth took it upon herself to go to work, truly as a "rookie", not knowing what would befall her. Would she be accepted, made fun of, or even bullied into quitting? How would she know where to go and what the rules are? Did she dress properly for the type of work? What would she do for lunch? Would there be insurance and benefits? Job security? Would she be working in the heat of the day breaking her back or her nails doing manual labor?

The Lord has given Ruth favor to find "the right Job", strength to perform this very manual labor, and the grit to hang with the "veteran" reapers through the heat of the day. Ruth is truly a hard worker; she barely took a break "**tarried a little in the house**". Ruth's humility is demonstrated in this verse as she simply asked for a chance to work.

There is no record of her calling in a favor to get the job or for it to be an easy "desk job".

Ruth works from morning till now (the whole day 6 AM to 6 PM). Jesus said "I must work the works of Him that sent me, while it is day: the night cometh, when no man can work" (John 9:4). Jesus is referring to the period of time after the Rapture of the body of Christ (1 Thess. 4:16-18) when no man can work because the night cometh (the tribulation). When Jesus died, the light of the world "went out" (Luke 23:44), the world was in darkness. The Church age is spoken of as a period of night time (darkness) as well, that will end with the sunrise (Millennium) (Mal. 4:2; 2 Pet. 1:19).

8 Then said Boaz unto Ruth, Hearest thou not, my daughter? Go not to glean in another field, neither go from hence, but abide here fast by my maidens:

"Hearest thou not, my daughter?" Boaz has "noticed" Ruth and taken an immediate liking to her. Boaz is going to offer her protection and see to it that her needs will be met cf. (vs. 15). Spiritually speaking, Jesus does the same for His children as Boaz did for Ruth. The Lord knows our needs and goes out of His way to spread some handfuls of purpose! "The Lord is nigh unto them that are of a broken heart; and saveth such as be of a contrite spirit" (Ps. 34:18).

"Hearest thou not, my daughter? Go not to glean in another field, neither go from hence" The Lord promises to meet all of our needs (Phil. 4:19). The Lord does not want His children to have to glean in other fields to make ends meet, but takes delight in answering our prayers (John 14:13).

The Lord does not want us to go into the "far country". The Lord's will was for Adam and Eve to remain in the garden, for the Jews to listen to Joshua and Caleb and go into the promised land, and for Israel to keep the promises that Solomon made at the dedication of the temple, which would have kept them in His field. However, the Lord's will was not done. The Lord knows what is best for us and as the Good Shepherd, would never lead us astray. We need to remain in the sheepfold and not wander into other fields and then we will have blessings, security, and peace (Ps. 119:165) instead of getting robbed by the world, Satan, and the thieves (John 10:10).

9 *Let* **thine eyes** *be* **on the field that they do reap, and go thou after them: have I not charged the young men that they shall not touch thee? and when thou art athirst, go unto the vessels, and drink of** *that* **which the young men have drawn.**

"*Let* thine eyes *be* on the field that they do reap" For best results, our eyes are to be fastened upon Jesus Christ (Heb. 12:2; Prov. 4:25), so that He can turn us from darkness to light and from the power of Satan unto God (Acts 26:18). Our eyes need to remain single to do the will of the Lord, otherwise they will let darkness into our body (Matt. 6:22) and we will be unprofitable.

Not only do our eyes need to be on the field we are reaping, but they need to be opened as well. We each have our own race to run and we are not competing against anyone but ourselves (Heb. 12:1), so we have to have our eyes on our field that we are reaping in, stay in our own lane, and strive lawfully, or we will not finish our race and be fruitful.

Unless our eyes are opened, we will trip and fall! Consider: (1.) Baalim's eyes had to be opened to see the Angel of the Lord (Num. 22-23) or he would have died. (2.) The Lord opened the eyes of John the Baptist to be able to see the Christ (John 1:29) and the Holy Spirit descend on Jesus. (3.) Elisha's eyes were opened to see the rapture of Elijah (2 Kings 2:12). (4.) A sinner's eyes have to be opened to see their sins in order to get saved cf. the Pharisees' eyes were opened, but they were blind (Matt.

23:24) and unsaved. (5.) Adam and Eve's eyes were opened to see their nakedness (Gen 3:7). (6.) The disciples' eyes had to be opened to see the risen Saviour (Luke 24). (7.) The two Jewish blind men in Matt. 9 had their eyes opened according to their faith. (8.) The Samarian woman had to have her eyes opened for supply and her salvation (John 4). (9.) Finally, the Lord opened Elisha's servant's eyes to see the salvation of the Lord's fiery horse army (2 Kings 6:17).

"have I not charged the young men that they shall not touch thee?" Boaz is ensuring Ruth's safety and is claiming her for his own. The Lord has claimed Israel, His wife, as His own and will not let anybody mess with her without consequences (Gen. 12). Jesus will not allow anyone to "kick" His bride (the Church) either (Acts 9:5).

The Lord protects His children from their enemies (Prov 16:17) and gives them sweet sleep (Prov. 3:24) in the midst of trying circumstances. No weapon formed against a child of the Lord can prosper unless the Lord allows it according to His will (Isa. 54:17) cf. Job. Satan could only go as far as the leash allowed that was placed upon him by God to manifest His purpose in Job's sufferings (Job 1:12). The Lord has placed a hedge about each of us (Job 1:10), though sometimes we can break free and go into another field, to ensure our protection and that nothing can touch us unless the Lord allows it to penetrate the safety net He has given us (John 10:28).

10 Then she fell on her face, and bowed herself to the ground, and said unto him, Why have I found grace in thine eyes, that thou shouldest take knowledge of me, seeing I *am* a stranger?

"Then she fell on her face, and bowed herself to the ground, and said unto him, Why have I found grace in thine eyes" Ruth falls prostrate to the one who has "saved" her. Again, Ruth is a stranger and a woman of color who deserves no special attention, but receives grace-unmerited favor. However, Ruth is reaping the blessing promised in Gen. 12 of helping a Jew, as she has been loyal to her Jewish mother-in-law Naomi. As mentioned before, Miphiboseth (see vs.1)-arguably one of the greatest pictures of grace in the Bible-fell at David's feet expecting to be killed, but was promoted instead. Another stranger and woman of color in the Bible, (the Syrophoenician woman), worshipped (fell down, begged, and called Jesus, Lord) Jesus and received a blessing of healing for her daughter (Matt. 15:25) at a time when Jesus was sent only to the lost sheep of the house of Israel.

For a more current example of grace, Dr. Ruckman tells a story of Frank LaGuardia from 1936.[39] "Frank LaGuardia, who was later the Governor of New York, was a probate judge. A poor man who was caught for stealing bread was brought to his court. Judge LaGuardia found the man guilty and fined him $10.00. But then he paid the fellow's fine himself. Then he fined the courtroom $50.00 for living in a town where a man had to steal bread. Then he took up a $47.50 collection from the courtroom to give the poor man. That's grace".

Ruth, like us, has received something she surely does not deserve. God gives us favor, puts us in the right field to work, has the right people paying attention to us, meets our need, then gives even our greed sometimes (vs16) by leaving the handfuls of purpose. The Lord keeps us safe and brings us home to a wedding (Rev. 19; Ruth 4:13).

11 And Boaz answered and said unto her, It hath fully been shewed me, all that thou hast done unto thy mother in law since the death of thine husband: and *how* thou hast left thy father and thy mother, and the land of thy nativity, and art come unto a people which thou knewest not heretofore.

---

39 (Ruckman Reference Bible 1492).

"It hath fully been shewed me" There is nothing covered (Luke 12:2) that shall not be revealed; God's providence is at work again. God has a way of putting us in circumstances that seem impossible with no end in sight, and then by working behind the scenes, delivers us with a strong hand.

Joseph seemed like a victim that was caught up in bad circumstances, but it was fully shown to his brethren, the second time, how the Lord moved behind the seemingly tragic scenes in his life to complete serenity. It was fully shown to Israel what a small shepherd boy named David could accomplish through his faith by killing Goliath. It was fully shown to Nebuchadnezzar how powerful God was by delivering Daniel from the lions' den and Shadrach, Meshach, and Abednego from the fiery furnace. All of these examples given were of ordinary people who obeyed God and left all the consequences to him. They expected no reward, and what they accomplished was "all in a day's work"; with God working on their behalf behind the scenes as He did for Ruth.

"hast left" Ruth has left all that she had to follow Naomi. Jesus asks us to leave all that we have and follow Him; some do and some do not. The rich young ruler (Matt. 19) did not, Peter left his business to follow Jesus (Matt. 4:19), Matthew left his comfortable accounting job to follow the Lord (Matt. 9:9), etc.

12 The LORD recompense thy work, and a full reward be given thee of the LORD God of Israel, under whose wings thou art come to trust.

"The Lord recompense thy work" Again, Ruth has taken care of a Jew and according to Gen. 12:3, God is going to recompense her in this life for doing so. In the O.T. if a Jew did right, God rewarded them with physical blessings in this life (Gen. 21:22; Deut. 28:1-14). However, the blessings change for the Jew in the N.T. cf. Rev. 2:9. In the N.T. God rewards Christians with spiritual blessings (Eph. 1:3) in this life and physical rewards at the Judgment Seat of Christ (1 Cor. 3:10-15). Ruth made her profession in Ch. 1:16-17 and has left her false gods to come to worship the Hebrew God of the Bible and take care of Naomi.

Hebrews 6:10 states "For God is not unrighteous to forget your work and labour of love, which ye have shewed toward His name, in that ye have ministered to the saints, and do minister" so Ruth's humility and service is going to be recompensed. "There is no honor before humility" (Prov. 15:33). It should be noted that Ruth's motives are sincere and not those of seeking some personal gain. "For whosoever exalteth himself shall be abased; and he that humbleth himself shall be exalted (Luke 14:11). Ruth simply wanted a better life to live and God to serve but has no idea of what the Lord has in store for her. If Ruth's motives were not right, she would have returned with Orpah instead of facing the unknown as a Jewish widow with a broke mother-in-law to care for.

During the tribulation, a Gentile (like Ruth) will have to take care of the Jew to make it into the Millennium and then be recompensed. Matt. 25:34-36 states "Then shall the King say unto them on his right hand, Come, ye blessed of my Father, inherit the kingdom prepared for you from the foundation of the world: For I was an hungred, and ye gave me meat: I was thirsty, and ye gave me drink: I was a stranger, and ye took me in: Naked, and ye clothed me: I was sick, and ye visited me: I was in prison, and ye came unto me". Spiritually speaking, it is better to be recompensed for doing right instead of sinning (Heb. 2:2).

"full reward" Boaz is asking the Lord to reward Ruth based upon her trust in him and great sacrifice to Naomi. Like Ruth, a Christian can receive a full reward by: keeping God's word (Rev. 3:8,10). Likewise, a Christian can lose a full reward by: (1.) being deceived (2 John 7), (2.)

by not having the right motive for service (1 Cor. 3:10-15), (3.) Having unconfessed sin (1 Cor. 11:31-32), (4.) Intemperance in your body (1 Cor. 9:24-27), (5.) not being a good testimony (2 John 8), (6.) by not sharing the gospel (Phil. 2:15-16).

13 Then she said, Let me find favour in thy sight, my lord; for that thou hast comforted me, and for that thou hast spoken friendly unto thine handmaid, though I be not like unto one of thine handmaidens.

"Let me find favour in thy sight, my lord" Though, Ruth has already found favour in Boaz's sight (vs. 11-12), she is now asking for more favour even though she is not a Jew and Boaz will give it (vs. 14-16). God's favour demonstrated through His strength is more than sufficient for His children (2 Cor. 12:9). Once saved, having ended the enmity with God (Rom. 8:7), He showers us with grace (Acts 4:33, 20:32; Rom. 5:2, 20; 2 Cor. 4:15, 9:14; Eph. 1:7; 1 Tim. 1:14) as Boaz favours Ruth.

"for that thou hast comforted me" The God of all comfort comforts His children (2 Cor. 1:3-5). While the World runs to alcohol, drugs, women, long hours at work, denial, blaming others, etc. to escape their problems, God gives Christians problems to then be able to comfort us which will edify us, increase our faith, and let us be an example to someone else less fortunate that He will place in our path to comfort.

It is a great comfort to know that a Christian will not go to Hell and eventually the Lake of Fire, that he will not be homeless for all of eternity but live in a mansion (John 14:1), and that all of our sorrow and tears will soon be wiped away (Rev. 21:4). It is also a comfort to know we are not alone in our despair and someone who loved us enough to die for us, answers our prayers and guides our paths home to heaven (New Jerusalem). The world offers no such comfort!

"though I be not like unto one of thine handmaidens" Boaz is practicing true religion by visiting the fatherless and widows in their affliction (James 1:27). Ruth is not a Jew; she is a Gentile stranger who is humbled and acting as a servant. She is claiming no rights as a Jewish widow, although, legally she could. The Lord claimed no rights either (Phil. 2:5-7), but became a servant and placed himself in subjection to the Father (1 Cor. 15:27-28).

A Christian has no "rights". A Christian that is concerned with his rights is not in proper subjection and is operating in the flesh. Oswald Chambers puts it this way, "One of the greatest proofs that you are drawing on the grace of God is that you can be humiliated without manifesting the slightest trace of anything but His grace".[40] A Christian must be in subjection at all times then and subsequently has no rights, because God has ordained whatever circumstances he is in (Phil. 4:11) to bring glory to His name (Rev. 4:11). If you claim rights, then you are rebelling against humiliation and God's providence for your circumstance. To be honest, the only rights human civilization has is to be arrested, die, and go to hell (Rom. 6:23), if we were to get what we deserve!

In the family setting the Lord should come first, followed by the husband, then the wife, and finally the children (Gen. 3:16; 1 Pet. 3:1, 5) to be in biblical subjection. In society, a Christian has to follow the laws of the government (Rom. 13:1-2) to be in biblical subjection and even a Christian's body has to be in subjection to the spirit (1 Cor. 9:27).

Satan refused to be in subjection to the Lord and was deposed (Isa. 14). The Jews, during the captivity, that placed themselves under subjection to Nebuchadnezzar through the word spoken by the prophet Jeremiah kept their lives as a prey (Jer. 21:9). Blessings come from being in biblical

---

40 Chambers, Oswald. My Utmost for His Highest. Barbour and Company, Inc.1935, June 26.

subjection, as seen in the lives of Daniel and Joseph for example. Daniel served under four different Gentile kings with a public service that spanned eighty years and was always placed second or third in their kingdoms by God. The Lord took Joseph through a thirteen-year field trip of pain and sorrow to be made second in command of the entire, known world.

Likewise, chaos will ensue for those who refuse to be in subjection to the Lord, as seen in the lives of Zedekiah (Jer. 52:9-10), who witnessed the death of his own children and had his eyes put out immediately afterwards for rebelling against God's order for subjection. Balaam (Num. 22) was cursed by God for trying to make money off cursing Israel, instead of being in subjection to the word given to him by the Lord. Finally, Jeroboam (1 Kings 13) contracted leprosy and was cursed by God, as well for not subjecting himself and his people to the proper place of worship, for fear of losing subjects, and for usurping the office of the priesthood by offering incense upon the altar.

14 And Boaz said unto her, At mealtime come thou hither, and eat of the bread, and dip thy morsel in the vinegar. And she sat beside the reapers: and he reached her parched *corn*, and she did eat, and was sufficed, and left.

"come thou hither" Boaz, like Jesus, is anticipating Ruth's needs that she may not have even considered herself. Jesus cares for even the fowls of the air and so will He not much more care for His children (Matt. 6). Boaz has "the bread" so he is in a position to take care of Ruth's physical needs. Jesus, the bread of life (John 6), takes care of our physical needs, but also advises us to seek Him for our spiritual needs as well (Deut. 8). Jesus said that we should come unto Him all that labor for rest for our souls (Matt. 11:28-30).

"vinegar" Vinegar is sour wine made from grape juice. Wine is a type of blood in the Bible (Deut. 32:14). At the Lord's supper, we drink new wine-which is grape juice (Isa. 65:8)-and eat bread (John 6). The new wine represents the Lord's blood and the bread represents His body (1 Cor. 11:26). So, Boaz is offering to Ruth, a Gentile, bread and a form of wine, allowing her to eat the food given to the servants when all he is commanded to do is allow her to glean; so she gets more than she deserves.

Concerning wine, in the Bible there is mention of old wine, new wine, wine, strong drink and mixed drinks. When the word wine is used by itself, one has to check the context to see if it is being used as new wine (grape juice Isa. 65:8) or old wine (fermented alcohol Prov. 23:30-31). When the words old wine or new wine is used, (rather than just wine) then it is made clear by that designation in the verse, which kind of wine it is; but the context has to be checked for proper interpretation (2 Tim. 2:15).

For example, many people always state that "Jesus turned water into wine" to excuse drinking; but what kind of wine did Jesus make? Nothing like a Bible to clear up a Bible question! Hab. 2:15 states "Woe unto him that giveth his neighbour drink, that puttest thy bottle to him, and makest him drunken also, that thou mayest look on their nakedness". Notice a woe is given, so Jesus could not have made alcohol because He would have violated the old testament law and would have committed a sin. If this was the case, then Jesus was not holy or sinless and therefore could not qualify as God.

Jesus made grape juice because Prov. 23:31 says "not to even look upon fermented wine" (red, leaves color in the cup, and moves itself through fermentation) much less to drink it and (vs. 32) states that it "bites like a serpent and stings like an adder". The sting has been the cause of many cases of physical/verbal abuse, broken homes, liver diseases, car accidents/deaths, and many a young woman losing her virginity, and more woes too numerous to list here.

Also, the law of first mention in Gen. 9:20 has wine connected to sin. Before the flood the atmospheric condition was different and thus Noah drank new wine, after the change in the atmosphere the grapes fermented, and Noah drank, got drunk and some sexual sin occurred as a result by his son Ham. Lot's daughters got him drunk using old wine to lie with him and commit incest, another sexual sin in Gen. 19:30. So, old wine is connected with nakedness and sexual sin. Also, when Moses came back with the ten commandments and heard the noise of war in the camp (rock music), the people were naked, drunk, making music and having sex orgies which is why the Lord killed approximately 23 thousand of them immediately (Exod. 32).

Alcohol always leads to sin. All references to fermented liquor in the Bible are given in a negative context. For example, David tried to get Uriah the Hittite drunk so he would go in and lie with his wife and get her pregnant to cover his sin of adultery with Bathsheba.

There is more Scripture in the Bible condemning the use of alcoholic beverages than will be found on the subjects of lying, adultery, swearing, cheating, hypocrisy, pride, or even blasphemy. In case you are not convinced yet that there is a difference in new and old wine, here are seventy-five biblical references about wine in the King James Bible given by Dr. Robert Teachout, a Semitic scholar who, in 1979, wrote his doctorate on The Use of Wine in the Old Testament, stated, "Alcohol is never approved by God in any amount for the obedient Christian".[41]

1. Genesis 9:20-26 - Noah became drunk; the result was immorality and family trouble.

2. Genesis 19:30-38 - Lot was so drunk he did not know what he was doing; this led to immorality.

---
41 scionofzion.com/drinking.htm.

3. Leviticus 10:9-11 - God commanded priests not to drink so that they could tell the difference between the holy and the unholy.

4. Numbers 6:3 - The Nazarites were told to eat or drink nothing from the grape vine.

5. Deuteronomy 21:20 - A drunken son was stubborn and rebellious.

6. Deuteronomy 29:5-6 - God gave no grape juice to Israel nor did they have intoxicating drink in the wilderness.

7. Deuteronomy 32:33 - Intoxicating wine is like the poison of serpents, the cruel venom of asps.

8. Judges 13:4, 7, 14 - Samson was to be a Nazarite for life. His mother was told not to drink wine or strong drink.

9. 1 Samuel 1:14-15 - Accused, Hannah said she drank no wine.

10. 1 Samuel 25:32-38 - Nabal died after a drunken spree.

11. 2 Samuel 11:13 - By getting Uriah drunk, David hoped to cover his sin.

12. 2 Samuel 13:28-29 - Amnon was drunk when he was killed.

13. 1 Kings 16:8-10 - The king was drinking himself into drunkenness when he was assassinated.

14. 1 Kings 20:12-21 - Ben-Hadad and 32 other kings were drinking when they were attacked and defeated by the Israelites.

15. Esther 1:5-12 - The king gave each one all the drink he wanted. The king was intoxicated when he commanded the queen to come.

16. Psalm 75:8 - The Lord's anger is pictured as mixed wine poured out and drunk by the wicked.

17. Proverbs 4:17 - Alcoholic drink is called the wine of violence.

18. Proverbs 20:1 - Wine is a mocker, strong drink is raging.

19. Proverbs 23:19-20 - A wise person will not be among the drinkers of alcoholic beverages.

20. Proverbs 23:21 - Drunkenness causes poverty.

21. Proverbs 23:29-30 - Drinking causes woe, sorrow, fighting, babbling, wounds with-out cause and red eyes.

22. Proverbs 23:31 - God instructs not to look at intoxicating drinks.

23. Proverbs 23:32 - Alcoholic drinks bite like a serpent, sting like an adder.

24. Proverbs 23:33 - Alcohol causes the drinker to have strange and adulterous thoughts, produces willfulness, and prevents reformation.

25. Proverbs 23:34 - Alcohol makes the drinker unstable.

26. Proverbs 23:35 - Alcohol makes the drinker insensitive to pain so he does not perceive it as a warning. Alcohol is habit forming.

27. Proverb 31:4-5 - Kings, Princes, and others who rule and judge must not drink alcohol. Alcohol pervert's good judgment.

28. Proverbs 31:6-7 - Strong drink could be given to those about to perish or those in pain. Better anesthetics are available today.

29. Ecclesiastes 2:3 - The king tried everything, including intoxicating drink, to see if it satisfied. It did not (Ecclesiastes 12:8).

30. Ecclesiastes 10:17 - A land is blessed when its leaders do not drink.

31. Isaiah 5:11-12 - Woe to those who get up early to drink and stay up late at night to get drunk.

32. Isaiah 5:22 - Woe to "champion" drinkers and "experts" at mixing drinks.

33. Isaiah 19:14 - Drunken men stagger in their vomit.

34. Isaiah 22:12-13 - The Israelites choose to drink; their future looks hopeless to them.

35. Isaiah 24:9 - Drinkers cannot escape the consequences when God judges.

36. Isaiah 28:1 - God pronounces woe on the drunkards of Ephraim.

37. Isaiah 28:3 - Proud drunkards shall be trodden down.

38. Isaiah 28:7 - Priests and prophets stagger and reel from beer and wine, err in vision, and stumble in judgment.

39. Isaiah 28:8 - Drinkers' tables are covered with vomit and filth.

40. Isaiah 56:9-12 - Drinkers seek their own gain and expect tomorrow to be just like today.

41. Jeremiah 35:2-14 - The Rechabites drank no grape juice or intoxicating wine and were blessed.

42. Ezekiel 44:21 - Again God instructed the priests not to drink wine.

43. Daniel 1:5-17 - Daniel refused the king's intoxicating wine and was blessed for it along with his abstaining friends.

44. Daniel 5:1 - Belshazzar, ruler of Babylon; led his people in drinking.

45. Daniel 5:2-3 - The king, along with his nobles, wives, and concubines, drank from the goblets which had been taken from God's temple.

46. Daniel 5:4 - Drinking wine was combined with praising false gods.

47. Daniel 5:23 - God sent word to Belshazzar that punishment would be swift for the evil he had committed.

48. Hosea 4:11 - Intoxicating wine takes away intelligence.

49. Hosea 7:5 - God reproves princes for drinking.

50. Joel 1:5 - Drunkards awake to see God's judgment.

51. Joel 3:3 - The enemy is judged for selling girls for wine.

52. Amos 2:8 - Unrighteous acts of Israel included the drinking of wine which had been taken for the payment of fines.

53. Amos 2:12 - Israel is condemned for forcing Nazarites to drink wine.

54. Micah 2:11 - Israelites are eager to follow false teachers who prophesy plenty of intoxicating drinks.

55. Nahum 1:10 - The drunkards of Nineveh will be destroyed by God.

56. Habakkuk 2:5 - A man is betrayed by wine.

57. Habakkuk 2:15 - Woe to him that gives his neighbor drink.

58. Habakkuk 2:16 - Drinking leads to shame.

59. Matthew 24:48-51 - A drinking servant is unprepared for his Lord's return.

60. Luke 1:15 - John the Baptist drank neither grape juice nor wine.

61. Luke 12:45 - Christ warned against drunkenness.

62. Luke 21:34 - Drunkenness will cause a person not to be ready for the Lord's return.

63. Romans 13:13 - Do not walk in drunkenness or immorality.

64. Romans 14:21 - Do not do anything that will hurt your testimony as a believer.

65. 1 Corinthians 5:11 - If a Christian brother is a drinker, do not associate with him.

66. 1 Corinthians 6:10 - Drunkards will not inherit the kingdom of God

67. Galatians 5:21 - Acts of the sinful nature, such as drunkenness, will prohibit a person from inheriting the kingdom of God.

68. Ephesians 5:18 - In contrast to being drunk with wine, the believer is to be filled with the Spirit.

69. 1 Thessalonians 5:6-7 - Christians are to be alert and self-controlled, belonging to the day. Drunkards belong to the night and darkness.

70. 1 Timothy 3:2-3 - Bishops (elders) are to be temperate, sober, and not near any wine.

71. 1 Timothy 3:8 - Deacons are to be worthy of respect and not drinkers.

72. 1 Timothy 3:11 - Deacons' wives are to be temperate and sober.

73. Titus 1:7-8 - An overseer is to be disciplined.

74. Titus 2:2-3 - The older men and older women of the Church are to be temperate and not addicted to wine.

75. 1 Peter 4:3-4 - The past life of drunkenness and carousing has no place in the Christian's life. (sic)

"reached" Reached is Elizabethan English meaning to give or hand over.

"parched corn" Parched corn is corn roasted "in the husk" (2 Kings 4:42) and rubbed in the hand to get the kernels out to eat (Deut. 23:25 cf. Luke 6:1).[42]

15 And when she was risen up to glean, Boaz commanded his young men, saying, Let her glean even among the sheaves, and reproach her not:

"reproach" Reproach means "address (someone) in such a way as to express disapproval or disappointment".[43] Boaz basically commands his men not to make fun of her, give her a hard time, or intimidate her. Boaz has set a hedge about Ruth (Job 1:10). No doubt if Ruth were reproached, she would have esteemed it greater than the riches she could have if she stayed in her land and married another heathen that could take care of only her physical needs (Heb. 11:26).

If a Christian is going to be reproached, it should be for the name of Christ (1 Pet.4:14), rather than for being slothful, unfaithful, for stealing, committing idolatry, riotous living, etc.

16 And let fall also *some* of the handfuls of purpose for her, and leave *them*, that she may glean *them*, and rebuke her not.

---

42 (Ruckman Ruth Commentary 370).
43 (Webster Dictionary).

"handfuls of purpose" The Lord knows all our need before we ever ask Him for help (Matt. 6:32). The Lord does exceeding abundantly above all the we ask (Eph. 3:20). The Lord gives **"handfuls of purpose"** to His children that have a grateful, instead of a greedy self-serving heart. The Lord delights in answering prayer (Luke 11:13).

The Lord gives **"handfuls of purpose"** also to the unsaved to woo them into salvation, in the form of being patient and longsuffering to their souls cf. (Rom. 9:22, 1 Pet. 3:20). The Lord, before I was saved, gave me a Christian mother who took me to church. He gave me a King James Bible instead of a book. He gave me an interest in going to church and Sunday School for the toys, prizes, candies, etc. that changed to craving the word of God. The Lord saved me from many accidents that could have left me severely handicapped, paralyzed, or even dead. The Lord put up with me many, many years, until finally I quit running and surrendered. The Lord had put a roof over my head, food in my stomach, clothes on my back, gave me good friends, schooling, grace to find jobs; and I never as much thanked Him until I realized that He had given me so many **"handfuls of purpose"**!

"rebuke" Satan rebukes the child of God constantly (Eph. 6:16). In our state (daily condition of sinning), this may be appropriate but, in our standing, (position as a saint) he has no authority to rebuke us (Rom. 8:33).

17 So she gleaned in the field until even, and beat out that she had gleaned: and it was about an ephah of barley.

"even" We have to work while we have light, because night cometh when no man can work (John 9:4) cf. notes in Ch. 2:8. Ruth worked the entire day from morning till evening cf. Matt. 20:1-16.

There is no retirement of God's calling for a Christian. I was at a doctor's office recently and the nurse saw my church shirt, understanding that I was a preacher, she hesitantly wondered if she could ask me a question. I replied "Of course you can". She asked "if I was retired (I guess I look old now) from preaching"? I said "no, you do not retire from the ministry any more than you quit breathing or eating"! She further stated that another patient had come into the office, who was a preacher as well, and when she saw this occupation listed on his chart, she asked him the same because the chart said that he was "retired". The patient told her that "preaching was just a job like anything else and he had "done it" for twenty years and was now retired". Her grandfather, being a Baptist preacher, apparently shared my view on the subject as well; there is no retirement when it comes to the ministry. So I guess she just wanted further confirmation besides what her grandfather had remarked on the situation.

"an ephah of barley" An ephah of barley is a little over a bushel and a bushel is three pints, according to Dr. Greg Estep.[44] Dr. Ruckman states "That was exceptional for one woman gleaning. It was obvious from the amount that she brought home that someone had given her a "break". see (vs.19).[45]

18 And she took *it* **up, and went into the city: and her mother in law saw what she had gleaned: and she brought forth, and gave to her that she had reserved after she was sufficed.**

"reserved after she was sufficed" Ruth had leftovers and brought them home to Naomi to share with. Boaz had made mention of Ruth taking care of Naomi (Ch. 2:11) and now Boaz is taking care of Ruth. Ruth is not looking out for herself, or saving up the leftovers to sell, or for a rainy day, she is trusting the Lord to meet the daily needs. 1 Tim. 5:4 states "But if any widow have children or nephews, let them learn

---
44 (Estep Ruth Class).
45 (Estep Ruth Class).

first to shew piety at home, and to requite their parents: for that is good and acceptable before God".

19 And her mother in law said unto her, Where hast thou gleaned to day? and where wroughtest thou? blessed be he that did take knowledge of thee. And she shewed her mother in law with whom she had wrought, and said, The man's name with whom I wrought to day *is* Boaz.

"Where hast thou gleaned to day?" Naomi asks Ruth where she has gleaned because she obviously was not expecting her to come home with so much grain. Gleaning, for the poor, is basically taking the small amount of leftover grain that fell to the ground, intentionally missed by the reapers for the poor's benefit "on purpose". Ruth has collected more than a "handful of purpose" cf. with the widow woman who fed Elijah by faith and under subjection to the word of God and was given oil a plenty (1 Kings 17) to meet her needs.

Spiritually, we shall give an account of our gleaning efforts as well to the Lord at the judgment seat of Christ (1 Cor. 3, 2 Cor. 5:10). Behold, today is the day of salvation (2 Cor. 6:2), so the question is, "Where have you gleaned today"? Are you gleaning for the Lord, for lost souls, and for your heavenly reward? What are you doing that is more important than gleaning? You say, "I will go tomorrow", but tomorrow may not come (Prov 27:1). You have said, "I will go", but you went not (Matt 21:30). Paul never missed an opportunity to glean (1 Cor. 9:19-23), even when he did not feel like it and things were against him (2 Cor. 11:28).

Biblically, the gleaning period of the Church age (Acts 1:8) started in Jerusalem with the gospel going to the Jew first. Then the gospel went to Judea to the Jews that were dispersed among the Gentiles. Next, the gospel was spread to the half-Jews in Samaria and finally sent to the Gentiles unto the utter most part of the earth.

This gleaning is illustrated in the book of Acts where God turns from the Jews to the Gentiles to spread the gospel in four major turning points. In Acts 7, the Lord closes the door to the Jews in Jerusalem. In Acts 13, the door closes for the Jews in Asia Minor. The door closes for the Jews in Europe in Acts 18. Finally, in Acts 28 the door closes for the Jew as they are dispersed worldwide and Jerusalem is destroyed in A.D. 70. Note however, that God will re visit the Jew in the time of Jacob's trouble (the tribulation) and restore Israel (Rom. 11) after this two thousand year pause.

Paul, the apostle to the Gentiles, also takes the gospel from the Jew to the Gentile as seen in the book of Acts. Originally the "kingdom gospel" was finally offered in Acts 7 with the stoning of Stephen and is replaced with "the gospel of the grace of God", see Acts 20:24. Paul preaches to the Gentiles solely from then on out as seen in Acts 13:46, 18:6, 28:28.

While teaching the book of Ruth, Dr. Estep asked, "Are you gleaning or grumbling?"[46] To be able to glean and not grumble, a Christian must maintain three visions, according to Dr. Ruckman.[47] (1.) The vision of the risen Christ (Acts 9:3-10). (2.) New Jerusalem (Rev. 21-22). (3.) The "harvest fields" (Matt. 9:37-38). A Christian that loses "the vision" of unsaved people in Hell (Matt. 13:49-50; Luke 16:22-31; Rev. 14:9-11; Rev. 20:11-15) is absolutely good for nothing!

20 And Naomi said unto her daughter in law, Blessed *be* he of the LORD, who hath not left off his kindness to the living and to the dead. And Naomi said unto her, The man *is* near of kin unto us, one of our next kinsmen.

"not left off his kindness to the living and to the dead" Now Naomi, like Ruth previously, has hit the jackpot! Naomi and Ruth came back broke, destitute, and with little to no hope-if any at all; but the Lord's providence

---

46 (Estep Ruth Class).
47 (Ruckman Reference Bible 893).

is at work again. Ruth went to work, found just the right field to work in, was treated with favour instead of like an outcast, and has now returned home to Naomi with more than expected from an honest day's work.

Naomi gives credit where credit is due; to the Lord, who gave her a second chance, forgiving her past mistake of leaving the house of bread to wander in the "gleaning fields of the World", and has now blessed both her and Ruth with his kindness.

I, probably just as you, have been in a place or two in my life, where I wandered around in the World as the prodigal son did; where I had no business being and felt that the Lord would never forgive me or take me back. The good news is that the Lord's mercies are renewed daily (Lam. 3:22-23), and that he does not hold a grudge (1 John 1:9). As the Lord welcomed the prodigal son back home, we, too, get, welcomed back under his limitless grace if we would but just ask, because "great is thy faithfulness" (Lam. 3:23).

21 And Ruth the Moabitess said, He said unto me also, Thou shalt keep fast by my young men, until they have ended all my harvest.

"keep fast" Ruth has job security, whereas Christians receive eternal security (Eph. 4:30). If we love our Saviour, we should keep fast by Him, His word, His people, His Church, and His will for our lives. We do not need to be gleaning in "other fields" or keeping so fast with the World that we are no good to the Church and cannot be distinguished between God or Satan's children.

"ended all my harvest" The end can prophetically refer to the tribulation, because people will have to work and endure for their salvation in that dispensation (Matt. 24).

22 And Naomi said unto Ruth her daughter in law, *It is* good, my daughter, that thou go out with his maidens, that they meet thee not in any other field.

"that they meet thee not in any other field" What field do you want the Lord to meet you in when He comes (Matt. 24:42)? Charles Stanley has stated many times that his mother used to warn him as a child; "Now Charles do not be doing anything that you would not want to be doing when the Lord comes"! I have heard many a mother says the same statement to their children over the years. Will the Lord meet you gleaning the fields that are ripe unto harvest, or burying your talents in the sand, so you can glean for your flesh (Matt. 25:18)? You cannot glean in another man's field either; you have to go glean in your own field (Rom. 15:20).

23 So she kept fast by the maidens of Boaz to glean unto the end of barley harvest and of wheat harvest; and dwelt with her mother in law.

"the end of barley harvest and of wheat harvest" The time period covered in verse 23 is about four months, which makes for a great courtship opportunity between Boaz and Ruth.

Dr. Ruckman states,[48] doctrinally, the time period of the barley harvest and the wheat harvest is the time period between Passover and Pentecost (see Lev. 23:5-22). This is the time between Christ's death and resurrection and the coming of the Holy Spirit in Acts 2. This is the time period given for the Rapture of the Bride in Song of Solomon 2:8-13.

---

48 (Ruckman Rith Commentary 378).

CHAPTER THREE

RUTH WOWS AND WAITS

3:1 Then Naomi her mother in law said unto her, My daughter, shall I not seek rest for thee, that it may be well with thee?

"seek rest" seek rest cf. Chapter 1:9. The rest spoken of here is plainly marriage. Yesteryear, the man would work a job to meet the financial needs of the family (1 Tim. 5:8) while the woman would stay at home and take care of the family (1 Tim. 5:14) She would cook, make clothes, clean the house, teach the children how to read the Bible and pray; etc. generally maintaining the family unit. "The good woman behind every successful man's back!" Naomi wants to help Ruth to be a stay-at-home mom and get her out of the manual labor pool before she is worn out. Probably, Naomi would like to be a grandmother also.

Today, though, most couples have to each work a full-time job just to make ends meet while the children attend public school, go to after school programs, do their homework, bathe and go to bed. It seems that today the government does more raising of children than parents do. In most modern families, having devotional time to the Lord around the dinner table does not exist. The Bible is not read or studied, there is no family prayer time, and board games are not even played anymore. Instead, everyone utilizes their personal electronic devices, further breaking down the structure of the family commonality, while becoming hermits under one roof and becoming more isolated.

Spiritually speaking, a Christian gets rest from Jesus (Matt. 11:28-29). This rest is also a type of the Church ceasing from works by accepting grace (Rom. 4:5, 10:4; Eph. 2:8-9).

2 And now *is* not Boaz of our kindred, with whose maidens thou wast? Behold, he winnoweth barley to night in the threshingfloor.

"Boaz of our kindred" Boaz, as mentioned previously in Chapter two, is near family. However, there is a family member who is closer (vs.12). Spiritually, we are all born in Adam's image and family unregenerated (Gen. 5:3), with Satan being our father (John 8:44) he is therefore a closer kinsman unless we get born again (John 3) into the image of God (John 1:12), thus making God our new father.

Boaz has to wait and see if the nearer family member will perform the part of the kinsman redeemer before he can claim and redeem Ruth. Jesus has purchased us with His propitiation offered on the cross. Jesus is longsuffering to see if we will accept His redemption or stay in Satan's family (2 Pet. 3:9).

"winnoweth barley to night in the threshingfloor" After the grain is harvested, it must be separated by being threshed. The grain would customarily be taken to a high place and be thrown into the air by a pitchfork or some other tool, (while the breeze was blowing), so that the grain and the chaff could be separated.

Similarly, Jesus has to separate the wheat from the chaff as well, at His harvest (Matt. 13:24-30). Jesus will have His fan in His hand and throughly purge His floor (Matt. 3:12). This winnowing process occurs at the end of the tribulation period, which is a time of darkness. Here Boaz is threshing in the night time, another period of darkness.

3 Wash thyself therefore, and anoint thee, and put thy raiment upon thee, and get thee down to the floor: *but* make not thyself known unto the man, until he shall have done eating and drinking.

"Wash thyself" The barley harvest season is ending and Ruth has been diligently working hard for about four months now (see notes on Ch. 2:23). Naomi is sending Ruth to meet Boaz and is preparing her by first taking a bath cf. Esther Ch. 2. (I personally take a bath every Saturday night, whether I need it or not!)

Water baptism cannot wash away our sins, even though there is bleach in the city water supply. It is done as an answer to a good conscience (1 Pet. 3:21). A Christian is commanded to be washed in the Word (John 15:3; Eph. 5:26; Titus 3:5). All of our righteousnesses are as filthy rags (Isa. 64:6) and it is not possible to ever wash ourselves enough (works) to gain entrance to heaven, but a Christian is commanded to live a clean life (2 Cor. 7:1; 1 Cor. 15:33; Jas. 4:8; 1 John 1:7, 9).

"anoint thee" First, Ruth is cleaning herself up by washing first and now by anointing herself with oils, spices, and perfumes to get Boaz's attention. Similar to Cinderella, Ruth is trading in the "mop and broom" for some "glass slippers", so she can be the envy of every woman at the festival. A Christian has to be washed in the blood to obtain the anointing of the Holy Ghost (1 Cor. 12:13; Rom. 6:4).

Opposite of Ruth, Daniel did not anoint his head with oil while trying to obtain an answer from the Lord to his prayer, (Dan. 10) but rather humbled himself for twenty-one days. Ps. 23 speaks of the shepherd anointing the sheep's head with oil. This anointing was done to ease the pain and hasten healing caused by cuts received on the sheep's head. It was also to applied to the nose area to keep worms and insects from laying eggs in the sheep's head, thus making them sick or killing even them.

A Christian has the anointing of the Holy Spirit (1 John 2:27) to guide him into the truth (John 16:13). We are to be filled with this anointing (Eph. 5:18). The Holy Ghost is given to every man by measure (John 3:34) and is only received one time (Col. 2:12), but we need to stir up this gift (2 Tim. 1:6) and get constant fillings to serve the Lord in a spiritual nature rather than a carnal one (Eph. 5:18).

"put thy raiment upon thee" Again, Ruth is going to put on the dress that will turn heads! You cannot go to the party without a dress or you will be cast out (Matt. 22:12). An unregenerated man's raiment will not get him into the party (heaven), either (Jas. 5:2).

Adam was originally clothed with light, until Satan "robbed" him of his garments in the garden. Adam tried to make his own garments but his effort was futile, so God intervened and supplied garments for him (Gen. 3).

A Christian is issued new raiment to wear for all of eternity for the marriage supper of the Lamb (Rev. 19:8) because Christians are washed in the blood; likewise, the tribulation saints are given ROBES that have been washed in the Lamb's blood (Rev. 6:11).

Ada R. Habershon suggests that A Christian should be "weaving for heaven".[49] There are three kinds of garments or raiment: (1.) Man-made garments that we are to put off (Isa. 59:6). (2.) God-given garments that

---

[49] Habershon, Ada R. A Study of the Types. Kregel Publications, 1957, pp. 68,70.

are put on us by God (Gen. 3:21). (3.) Spirit-wrought garments that are worked through us (Rom. 13:14).

Concerning man-made garments: (1.) They are original, but not sufficient (Gen. 3:7). (2.) They are natural, but not clean (Zech. 3). (3.) They are smart, but useless (Isa. 64:6). (4.) They are mended, but made worse (Mark 2:21).

Even the Lord has "garments" and "a vesture". Dr. Ruckman states,[50] concerning Heb. 1:12, that God's clothes are the physical universe (Psa. 104:2,6; Isa. 40:22) and He is going to take them off. This event is described in 2 Pet. 3:10-11 and Rev. 20:11.

Note that God's clothes are called "a garment" and "a vesture" in this passage. These are the same words applied to the clothes taken off His Son when He was crucified naked. Imagine the horror of those people who looked on Jesus Christ when He was naked at Calvary when they see His Father at the white throne Judgment and the son clothed in righteousness and light!

4 And it shall be, when he lieth down, that thou shalt mark the place where he shall lie, and thou shalt go in, and uncover his feet, and lay thee down; and he will tell thee what thou shalt do.

"mark the place" Ruth is to seek after Boaz and mark the place where he lies. There are many people and distractions at the party, so Ruth must be diligent in her search.

A star, Michael the archangel (Rev. 1:20) "marked" the place where Jesus was born (Matt. 2:9). Christians are to mark them which cause division (Rom. 16-17). In the tribulation, the Lord will mark His servants (Rev. 7:3), just as satan will mark his children (Rev. 14:9,11). Cain (Gen. 4:15) was the first person in the Bible to be marked.

---

50 (Ruckman Reference Bible 1599).

"uncover his feet" In accordance with Deut. 25:8-10, as revealed to Ruth by Naomi, Ruth is instructed to lay at Boaz's feet until she is told what to do. If Boaz accepts the position of the kinsman redeemer, all is well. If not, then she is to lose his shoe from off of his foot and spit in his face.

5 And she said unto her, All that thou sayest unto me I will do.

"I will do" Again, Ruth, not being a Jew or understanding the customs, follows Naomi's instructions. Samuel followed all that the Lord told him to do and did not let any of His words fall to the ground (1 Sam. 3:19). "A Christian that is 99% obedient is 100% disobedient". Saul did not do all that the Lord told him to do and, lost his office of king, his life, and even his salvation (1 Sam. 15:22, 16:14).

6 And she went down unto the floor, and did according to all that her mother in law bade her.

"down unto the floor" Ruth humbles herself by going down to the floor and is about to get promoted, married, and fulfill God's will for her life. Cf. with Jonah who goes down to Joppa, down in the ship, down into the sides of the ship, and down into the belly of the whale (Jonah 1-2) while running from the Lord's will for his life in disobedience.

7 And when Boaz had eaten and drunk, and his heart was merry, he went to lie down at the end of the heap of corn: and she came softly, and uncovered his feet, and laid her down.

"drunk" Drunk is used as a verb in this passage and is the past tense of drink. (See notes on Ch. 2:14) Boaz, a type of Christ, was not drunk by drinking fermented alcohol.

8 And it came to pass at midnight, that the man was afraid, and turned himself: and, behold, a woman lay at his feet.

"And it came to pass at midnight, that the man was afraid" It is midnight and Boaz is sound asleep. He wakes to find a stranger at his feet, afraid in the sense of being startled and shocked.

"at midnight" Here is a type of the Rapture; the Lord gathering the Church unto Himself (1 Thess. 4:16-18) as Ruth lays at the feet of Boaz waiting for him to spread his skirt over her gathering her unto himself, protecting her and preparing for a marriage feast (Rev. 19). The Lord will come in the clouds to take his bride home for a wedding feast.

The Rapture consists of Jesus taking a Gentile bride from earth in a moment to be judged at the judgment seat of Christ (1 Cor. 3) and then to the marriage supper of the lamb (Rev. 19). Other types in the Bible of taking a Gentile wife would include:

1. Joseph taking Asenath (Gen. 41:45).
2. Solomon taking his wife (Song of Songs 2:10). *Solomon had many Gentile wives.
3. Ahasuerus taking Esther (Esther 2:17).
4. Abraham taking Hagar (Gen. 16).
5. Isaac taking Rebekah (Gen. 24).
6. David taking Abigail and others (1 Sam. 25).
7. Moses taking Zipporah (Exod. 2:21).
8. Sampson taking a woman from Timnath (Judges 14).

Some other types of, or references to, the Rapture illustrated in the Bible are as follows:

1. Gen. 5:24. Enoch being translated before Noah's flood (wrath). There were three groups that faced Noah's flood; those that were removed before the flood (like Enoch), those that were saved through the flood like Noah and his family, and those that faced the wrath of God and perished in the flood like the population of the earth did.

2. Gen. 19:22-23. The removal of Lot before the destruction of Sodom and Gomorrah (wrath).

3. Gen. 23:4. Sarah, as Israel, represents the "Father's" bride who is put away for about two thousand years, while "the son" (Isaac) is getting him a Gentile bride.[51] Dr. Ruckman.

4. Matt. 24:54. A type of the Holy Spirit's work in this age in the night, with the Rapture occurring in the morning.

5. Exod. 3:20. Devotionally, the Church leaving the world at the Rapture.

6. Exod. 13:19. Joseph, the greatest type of Christ in the Bible, must not leave one of his bones in the World (Egypt), as not one bone of Christ was left on this earth, nor will there be left one bone of any believer after the Rapture occurs.

7. Zeph. 2:3. The Church will be hid from wrath in the day of the Lord's anger. See also 1 Thess. 5:9 where the Church is not appointed to wrath.

8. Gen. 22:19-24, 63. Isaac's absence after the offering, as the Church is absent after Christ's offering on Calvary.

9. Dan. 5. Daniel's absence from the furnace, a type of tribulation.

---

51 (Ruckman Reference Bible 46).

10. Isa. 26:19-21. The Lord's people are hid in the chambers for a little moment until the indignation be past.

11. Ps. 27:5. In the time of trouble the Church will be hid in the pavilion, in secret, set upon a Rock.

12. John 14:3. Our place is prepared and the Lord comes for His bride.

13. Prov. 11:8. The Church is Raptured and antichrist comes in his name.

14. Further verses concerning the Rapture are: Josh. 2:19, 1 Cor. 15:1-53; Rom. 8:19; 1 Cor. 1:7-8, 1 Cor. 16:22; Phil. 3:20,21; Col. 3:4; 1 Thess. 1:10, 2:19, 5:9, 5:23; 2 Thess. 2:1; 1 Tim. 4:1; Titus 2:13; Heb. 9:28; James 5:7-9; 1 Pet. 1:7,13; 1 Jn 2:28-32; Jude 21, Rev. 2:25, 3:10.

There is a distinct difference between the Rapture and the Second Coming. For example, The Lord will come first in the air FOR His bride before coming on the ground WITH His bride: "shall be caught up together with them in the clouds to meet the Lord in the air" (1 Thess. 4:16).

The Rapture differs from the Second Coming of Christ in many aspects; The Rapture-Translation of Believers only, translated saints go to heaven, the Earth not judged, is imminent, affects believers only, occurs before day of wrath, no reference to Satan mentioned, Jesus comes for His own, comes in the air, claims His bride, only His own see Him, great tribulation begins, happens in the twinkling of an eye; verses, The Second Coming: No translation is involved, translated saints return to Earth, the Earth is judged, follows definite predicted signs, affects all men on earth, concludes day of wrath, Satan is bound, Jesus comes with His own, comes to Eearth-not clouds, comes with His bride, all eyes see

Him, Millennium begins, the Advent is an extended activity and not a momentary occurrence like the Rapture.

Also, the apostle John is singled out from the other apostles as a type of the church and was the disciple "whom Jesus loved" (John 13:23) and the body of Christ is referred to Christs "beloved" (Eph. 1:6), John is the only disciple whom Jesus promised would see His bodily return (John 21:22-23). So again, the Rapture is differentiated from the Second Advent.

The doctrine of imminence; the Rapture can happen at any time and is not contingent on any circumstance: Phil. 3:20; Titus 2:13; Heb. 9:28; 1 Thess. 1:10, 4:16, 5:6; Rev. 22:20, whereas the second coming has predicted steps (Titus 2:13, Dan. 2:44-45).

Chuck Missler[52] states that there are seven Raptures in the Bible: (1.) Enoch. Gen. 5:24; Heb. 11:5. (2.) Elijah. 2 Kings 2:1, 11. (3.) Jesus. Mark 16:19; Acts 1:9-11; Rev. 12:5. (4.) Phillip. Acts 8:39. (5.) Paul. 2 Cor. 12:2-4. (6.) Body of Christ. 1 Thess. 4:17. (7.) John. Rev. 4:1.

9 And he said, Who *art* thou? And she answered, I *am* Ruth thine handmaid: spread therefore thy skirt over thine handmaid; for thou *art* a near kinsman.

"thy skirt" Skirt is defined in 1 Sam 15:27, 24:4 as a garment that hung down from the waist of a robe or coat. During biblical times, men often wore skirts or mantles over their clothing that would serve as a covering or shelter from water or sand storms, among other uses.

In Judges 4:18, Jael covered Sisera with a mantle before killing him. Elijah smote the waters with his mantle in 2 Kings 2:8, causing them to divide so he could pass through on dry land. Ezra, Job and other books further demonstrate the use of a skirt or mantle. In modern times, skirts are still worn by men in countries such as Scotland, Japan, and China for customary tradition mostly.

---

52 youtube.com/watch?v=SFTr53H9GIA.

"spread thy skirt over thine handmaid" Ezekiel 16:8 states "Now when I passed by thee, and looked upon thee, behold, thy time was the time of love; and I spread my skirt over thee, and covered thy nakedness: yea, I sware unto thee, and entered into a covenant with thee, saith the Lord God, and thou becamest mine". (See notes vs.8). Ruth is telling Boaz to do his part of the kinsman redeemer by spreading his skirt over her. Basically, Ruth is proposing to Boaz and is offering him a chance to reclaim her by this token gesture, which will cover and protect her while entering into a marriage covenant. The request is pure and symbolical with no intent for fornication or otherwise evil occurrent.

"for thou art a near kinsman" There is a closer kinsman (see note on Ch. 3:2). For a kinsman to qualify as a redeemer, there are three requirements, according to Dr. Estep.[53] (1.) The near kinsmen, cannot be from outside the family. (2.) They must be willing to redeem and must meet all the qualifications before redemption can occur. (3.) Be able to redeem, financially and otherwise.

10 And he said, Blessed *be* thou of the LORD, my daughter: *for* thou hast shewed more kindness in the latter end than at the beginning, inasmuch as thou followedst not young men, whether poor or rich.

"followedst not young men, whether poor or rich" Obviously, Ruth, being an attractive woman, had her choice of younger and possibly even wealthier men to choose from. Based on her profession in Ch. 1:16-18, Ruth was sincere, single-minded and had her eyes focused "right on" (Prov 4:25) to finding a husband, taking care of Naomi, and having a relationship with the God of Israel.

---

53 (Estep Ruth Class).

11 And now, my daughter, fear not; I will do to thee all that thou requirest: for all the city of my people doth know that thou *art* a virtuous woman.

"**I will do to thee all that thou requirest**" "Slow and steady wins the race"! Ruth's determination, patience, and hard work has finally paid off. Not being a "gold digger", but rather having a pure heart, has placed Ruth in a position to be promoted by God; earning her a place in history and giving her rest, both physically and matrimonially. The bath, anointing, and dress did not hurt either, but what Boaz sees is a virtuous woman whom he can trust and just happens to be as beautiful on the outside as on the inside.

"**for all the city of my people doth know that thou *art* a virtuous woman**" Many people have said in one fashion or another that "reputation is what others think of you, but character is who you really are"! Further, your character is what you are alone in the dark with, only God knowing the very deepest recesses of your mind.

Ruth has stood out like a sore thumb-in a good way! Ruth's example has gotten the crowds talking, earned her the respect of the "townsfolk"; and surely exceeded all of Naomi's wildest expectations considering Orpah's actions of turning back to take care of herself. The Bible speaks of a woman like this in Prov. 31, called the virtuous woman. Ruth is the only woman in the Bible to have had this honor said about her.

According to Dr. Ruckman,[54] there turns out to be twelve kinds of women in Proverbs: "a fair woman" (Prov. 11:22), "a gracious woman" (Prov. 11:16), "a whorish woman" (Prov. 6:26), "an odious woman" (Prov. 30:23), "an adulterous woman" (Prov. 30:20), "a brawling woman" (Prov. 21:9), "a strange woman" (Prov. 2:16), "an evil woman" (Prov. 6:24), "a contentious and angry woman" (Prov. 21:19), "a foolish woman" (Prov. 9:13), a "wise woman" (Prov. 14:1), and the "virtuous woman" (Prov. 12:4).

---

54 (Ruckman Reference Bible 895).

12 And now it is true that I *am thy* near kinsman: howbeit there is a kinsman nearer than I.

"**nearer than I**" (See notes on vs. 2).

13 Tarry this night, and it shall be in the morning, *that* if he will perform unto thee the part of a kinsman, well; let him do the kinsman's part: but if he will not do the part of a kinsman to thee, then will I do the part of a kinsman to thee, *as* the LORD liveth: lie down until the morning.

"**Tarry this night, and it shall be in the morning**" (See notes on Ch. 2:7). John 9:5 states "As long as I am in the world, I am the light of the world". Since the lights went out when Jesus was crucified on the cross (Luke 23:44), and "the light of the world" will soon be leaving, then nighttime (6 PM to 6 AM) can picture the Church age. If this type is used, then the sunlight would be the Millennium.

Doctrinally, there are four watches in the Jewish night representing 500 years apiece in the Church age; Christ's departure being as the sun going down (John 11:9-10) and His return as the sun coming up (Mal. 4:2), according to Dr. Ruckman.[55] The first watch ends at 9 P.M. with Pope Gregory the Great; the second watch ends at midnight with the Crusades; the third ends at 1500 A.D. with Martin Luther (1520); the Christian is now in the fourth watch and is awaiting the RISE of "the Day star" (2 Pet. 1:19).

The sun coming up in the morning after night (Isa. 21:11-12,12; Mal. 4:2; Matt. 24:43; 1 Thess. 5:1-6) is mentioned in the scriptures as the coming of the King in glory for His thousand-year reign on earth at Jerusalem.

Ruth must tarry this night to see what will become of her situation in the morning, but Boaz has made clear, that if it is at all possible, he will do the part of the kinsman redeemer.

---
55 Ruckman, Peter S. Matthew Commentary. BB Bookstore, 1978, p. 560.

14 And she lay at his feet until the morning: and she rose up before one could know another. And he said, Let it not be known that a woman came into the floor.

"**And she lay at his feet**" Ruth laid at Boaz's feet with her marriage proposal being accepted on the grounds that nearer kinsman would forfeit his allowance; not with him and not carnally as in the definition of the word "know". Boaz is a type of the Lord Jesus Christ. Boaz is interested in obtaining this virtuous woman for his wife, not committing fornication.

"**Let it not be known that a woman came into the floor**" Boaz has done nothing wrong, but does not want to give the appearance of having done evil, and so he gives Ruth these instructions to abstain from all appearances of evil (1 Thess. 5:22). Dr. David Walker[56] has used an illustration in some of his sermons to demonstrate abstaining from all appearances of evil. He states "there would be nothing wrong with me taking a whiskey bottle, cleaning it out, filling it with water and putting it behind the pulpit to drink water from while preaching, but it would not be proper or appropriate to do so and would give the wrong appearance and offend the brethren"!

15 Also he said, Bring the vail that *thou hast* upon thee, and hold it. And when she held it, he measured six *measures* of barley, and laid *it* on her: and she went into the city.

"**he measured six *measures* of barley, and laid *it* on her**" Boaz has made an oath to the Lord (see Vs. 13). He is now making an earnest payment to Ruth to show his intentions of keeping his oath cf. The Holy Ghost is given as an earnest payment until the redemption of the believer's body (2 Cor. 1:22).

---

56 Walker, David. Various sermons preached at Calvary Baptist Church, 2009-2018.

"Laid it on her" is still used in today's vernacular. Have you ever heard someone say "lay it on me" while holding out a plate to get more food, or in a card game, for example?

"she went into the city" According to some critics, there is a controversy as to whether the verse is stating that Boaz or Ruth went into the city depending on different editions of the KJV. The Cambridge version states that she (Ruth) went into the city. Rather than make a lengthy explanation in reference to this supposed contradiction, let me state that whether the text stated that "he" or "she" went into the city, then both would be correct as they both go into the city (Ruth in Vs. 16; Boaz in Ch. 4:1).

16 And when she came to her mother in law, she said, Who *art* thou, my daughter? And she told her all that the man had done to her.

"she came to her mother in law" Yep, that's what the result was of the contradiction mentioned in Vs. 15, she went into the city where Naomi was.

"Who *art* thou, my daughter?" Has Naomi suffered from Alzheimer's or dementia overnight? Of course not! Naomi is enquiring as to Ruth's marital status. "Did Ruth get married last night" is what Naomi is asking.

Concerning marriage, a Christian should first come together spiritually, meaning a Christian should marry another Christian, for best results (1 Cor. 7:28). Secondly, the couple should come together socially and have some shared interests in common. Lastly, a virgin Christian should come together with another virgin Christian, and "know" each other (physically), then remain married for the rest of their lives, for best results.

Does a proposal make you married? No. Does getting a marriage license make you married? No. Does having a marriage ceremony make you married? No. Does putting on a ring make you married? No. So, what exactly constitutes marriage, then? According to the Bible, it is flesh joining flesh (Gen. 2:24; Matt. 19:5-6; Rom. 7:2-3; 1 Cor. 6:16; Eph. 5:31).

"And she told her all that the man had done to her" Boaz "staked his claim", made an oath to the Lord, and made a down payment on his vow. That is all that Boaz did. I am sure there was some prayer about "thank you, Lord, for this beautiful, hardworking, virtuous woman, who took care of Naomi instead of abandoning her, and came back to possibly face ridicule, and work all day in the heat of the sun, and kept her eyes where they belonged, and did not go out and waste her income on (shopping) and did not flirt with every young, good-looking guy that came along, but came here and proposed to me because I was too nervous and insecure after four months to pop the question. Well, that is about it. Good night, Lord". But, Boaz did not "know" (marry) Ruth, yet!

17 And she said, These six *measures* **of barley gave he me; for he said to me, Go not empty unto thy mother in law.**

"Go not empty unto thy mother in law" A Christian should not go home to Heaven empty either. The Lord has given every child gifts (Matt. 7:11; Rom. 12:6; 1 Cor. 12:31; Eph. 4:8; Heb. 2:4) that should be used to bring glory and honour to His name (Rev. 4:11).

18 Then said she, Sit still, my daughter, until thou know how the matter will fall: for the man will not be in rest, until he have finished the thing this day.

"Sit still" Ruth is, no doubt, very excited. Maybe, Ruth is remembering how-just a few months ago-she was alone in the World, without hope or God, and an alien to the common wealth of Israel (Eph. 2:12). She was destitute, having no answers or even a plan, but to follow an elderly Jew back to her people, which were her enemies. In such a short amount of time, the Lord has prospered Ruth and Naomi with material and spiritual blessings. Ruth is about to retire from manual labor and become a mother, a wife, and a very important person in the Bible for all of eternity.

Devotionally, the passage illustrates a sinner that is relying on the finished work of Jesus for salvation, instead of their own works. Ruth called upon Boaz by uncovering his skirt; and a Christian has to call upon Jesus for salvation (Rom 10:13). Boaz now has to do his part, as Jesus did (Heb. 10:12).

"the man will not be in rest, until he have finished the thing this day" Again, Boaz is excited and will not rest until his mission is accomplished cf. Titus (2 Cor. 8:16). Jesus had a task to accomplish as well (John 4:34). Jesus finished His task (John 19:30).

CHAPTER FOUR

RUTH GETS WEDDED

4:1 Then went Boaz up to the gate, and sat him down there: and, behold, the kinsman of whom Boaz spake came by; unto whom he said, Ho, such a one! turn aside, sit down here. And he turned aside, and sat down.

"the gate" In biblical times, the gate was where business was conducted; official or unofficial, and decisions were made. Examples found in any concordance include, but is not limited to: (1.) Lot serving in some governmental manner sitting at the gate (Gen.19:1). (2.) Absalom (2 Sam. 15:2) advancing his political career by mutiny at the gate. (3.) Moses (Exod. 32:26) drew the line in the sand as far as who was on the Lord's side at the gate. (4.) Josh. 20:4 states the gate was the place for a person seeking refuge to apply for asylum. (5.) Acts 12:10 defines the gate as an iron structure that leads into the city. (6.) Christ suffered without the gate (Heb. 13:12). (7.) Sampson carried away the doors of the gate (Judges 16:3).

"Ho, such a one" According to Dr. Estep[57], the nearer kinsman's name is not mentioned because he is not important, since he does not redeem

---
57 (Estep Ruth Class).

Ruth. He is more interested in saving his good name and not marring his inheritance, and in so doing, loses his name. (see notes on Ch. 1:8). Cf. John 12:25 "He that loveth his life shall lose it; and he that hateth his life in this world shall keep it unto life eternal".

2 And he took ten men of the elders of the city, and said, Sit ye down here. And they sat down.

"**ten men of the elders of the city**" Naomi is correct; Boaz is wasting no time trying to keep his word and marry Ruth. Again, "**ten**" is a Gentile number (see notes on Ch. 1:4), but with the addition of Boaz and the nearer kinsman redeemer, there are twelve participants in the business deal. "In the mouth of two or three witnesses shall every word be established" (2 Cor. 13:1). Hence, a twelve-man jury today for trial on serious criminal offences.

Twelve represents Israel in the Bible. There are twelve tribes, apostles, stones in the high priest breastplate. Larkin[58] states further that there are twelve cakes of shewbread; wells of water at Elim; spies sent into Canaan; Joshua places twelve stones in the river bed of Jordan; Elijah built an altar of twelve stones; Solomon's "Molten Sea" stood on twelve brass oxen; Jesus visited the temple at twelve years of age: Jesus could have requested twelve legions of angels. Then there was the woman who was diseased for twelve years, and the twelve-year-old daughter Jairus. In the Book of Revelation, we read of the woman with a crown of twelve stars, and that the New Jerusalem has twelve gates, at the gates twelve angels; that is has twelve foundations, and in them the names of the twelve Apostles of the Lamb; that its trees bear twelve manner of fruits; that lieth foursquare and measures twelve thousand furlongs on a side, and that the height of the wall is 144 cubits, or 12x12. We are also told

---

58 (Larkin Dispensational Truth 173).

that in the "Regeneration" the twelve apostles shall sit on twelve thrones judging the twelve tribes of Israel (Matt. 19:28).

3 And he said unto the kinsman, Naomi, that is come again out of the country of Moab, selleth a parcel of land, which *was* **our brother Elimelech's:**

"**selleth a parcel of land**" Boaz gets right to the point, as he will not rest until his business is finished (Ch. 3:18). According to 1 Kings 21:1-4, Naboth, the Jezreelite, was not able to sell his vineyard (**parcel of land**) to King Ahab, who desperately wanted it; as explained in Num. 36:7-11. The idea was to preserve the land between each tribe as given by the Lord in the book of Joshua and not let anyone sell out their inheritance and go without. An example today would be the larger corporations acquiring smaller ones to the point that they become a monopoly, giving the consumer poorer customer service and loss of competitive choices to seek a better company, if the service being received is not sufficient to the customers' expectations.

Devotionally speaking, a Christian should not sell or lose his inheritance for earthly temporal choices, either. Col. 3:23-25 states "And whatsoever ye do, do it heartily, as to the Lord, and not unto men; Knowing that of the Lord ye shall receive the reward of the inheritance: for ye serve the Lord Christ. But he that doeth wrong shall receive for the wrong which he hath done: and there is no respect of persons".

There is a heavenly inheritance received at salvation, (Gal. 3:19-29) and there is an earned inheritance separate from salvation, according to 1 Pet. 1:4. The Millennial inheritance (2 Tim. 2:12) is an earned reward as is the rewards given at the Judgment Seat of Christ (1 Cor. 3:12).

A Christian can earn gold, which symbolizes deity and is a reward for worshipping Jesus Christ as God. Silver can also be earned by telling people how to get saved and is the price of redemption (Num. 3:47-49).

Finally, precious stones-which are people-(Mal. 3:17, Zech. 9:16, Prov. 31:10) can be laid up in heaven, as well as a reward for winning souls to Christ (Jas. 5:20).

4 And I thought to advertise thee, saying, Buy *it* before the inhabitants, and before the elders of my people. If thou wilt redeem *it*, redeem *it*: but if thou wilt not redeem *it*, *then* tell me, that I may know: for *there is* none to redeem *it* beside thee; and I *am* after thee. And he said, I will redeem *it*.

"**I will redeem** *it*" *Prov. 18:13 states* "He that answereth a matter before he heareth it, it is folly and shame unto him". The nearer kinsman has hastily agreed to make the required purchase without hearing the rest of the matter; which includes a Gentile widow and a requirement of marriage as well. He is acting upon his lusts to enlarge his riches (Jas. 4:2).

Does not this nearer kinsman want to know where the land is located or what condition it is in before he writes a check and becomes a "slum lord"? After working with his very close friend, Hiram, for twenty years, King Solomon, the wisest person that ever lived, gave Hiram twenty cities as a gift (1 Kings 9:12) and they pleased him not! This nearer kinsman reminds me of the first man that was invited by the Lord to the great supper (Luke 14:18) that said "I have bought a piece of ground, and I must needs go and see it; I pray thee have me excused" (I wonder if the two are related or at the very least separated by only six degrees?). Who buys land without seeing it first?

5 Then said Boaz, What day thou buyest the field of the hand of Naomi, thou must buy *it* also of Ruth the Moabitess, the wife of the dead, to raise up the name of the dead upon his inheritance.

"**buyest the field**" Here is a picture of Jesus Christ buying the field that contains hidden treasure (Matt. 13:44) of Jews and Gentiles alike that become the Church, His bride and His treasure! The nearer kinsman redeemer is not interested in redeeming a Gentile and raising up half breed Jews like the Samaritans. His mouth wrote a check that his flesh cannot cash! Jesus had to buy all the "trash" (Isa. 64:6) that came with the field and then do a lot of "repairs" to conform us to His image (Rom. 8:29).

6 And the kinsman said, I cannot redeem *it* for myself, lest I mar mine own inheritance: redeem thou my right to thyself; for I cannot redeem *it*.

"**I cannot redeem *it* for myself**" (see notes Ch. 3:2) As mentioned earlier, that Satan is a nearer kinsman considering we are born in the image of Adam, and not of God's. This is because Adam fell in the garden (Gen. 3). Dr. Ruckman[59] presents another possible type: "the picture here is between God the Father and God the Son. Boaz of course is a picture of Jesus Christ-God the Son. That being the case, there would only be one "kinsman" nearer who could redeem us; that would be God the Father. God could not redeem the Gentiles personally Himself because He already had a bride who was His inheritance-the nation of Israel (see Deut. 32:9; Ps. 28:9, 33:12, 78:62, 94:14; and Hos. 1-3). Ruth is a type of the Gentile bride of Christ. If God the Father had taken "Ruth" to be His wife, He would have violated what He Himself said in Deut. 23:3-6".

Now, this is not just a racial or national thing; it goes all the way into eternity, where the saved Jews of the Old Testament and from the Tribulation get the new earth as an inheritance (Rom. 4:13), while the body of Christ gets the New Jerusalem (Rev. 21:9). While the Jews and Gentiles may be one in Christ spiritually right now (Eph. 2:11-17), the "marriage" (Eph. 5:25-32) is not "consummated" (Rev. 19:7-9) until the

---
59 (Ruckman Ruth Commentary 394).

"nearer kinsman" (God the Father) takes His shoe off (vs. 7 cf. Deut. 25:10) "over Edom" (Ps. 60:8, 108:9) in the Tribulation.

"**lest I mar mine own inheritance**" The Jews reject God the Father in the O.T. (1 Sam. 8), God the Son in the N.T. (John 19), and God the Holy Spirit (Acts 7). Even after being completely rejected, Jesus chose to "**mar**" Himself to redeem lost sinners (Ps. 129:3; Isa. 50:6, 53:4-5).

"**I cannot redeem *it***" This is a picture of what the World, good works, and religion cannot redeem. They can not redeem anything, not even the time (Eph. 5:16). The nearer kinsman is married to a Jewess; Boaz is single and can marry Ruth, without violating the rights of a Jewish wife.

7 Now this *was the manner* in former time in Israel concerning redeeming and concerning changing, for to confirm all things; a man plucked off his shoe, and gave *it* to his neighbour: and this *was* a testimony in Israel.

"**a man plucked off his shoe**" This custom, mentioned in Ch. 3, is a fulfillment of Deut. 25:9. All things must be done decently and in order (1 Cor. 14:40). Ps. 60:8 states that God will cast out His shoe over Edom. (There is no intelligible exegesis for this verse given to anyone thus far by the Holy Ghost).

8 Therefore the kinsman said unto Boaz, Buy *it* for thee. So he drew off his shoe.

"**Buy *it***" Nothing is free in life except for salvation (Isa. 55:12; Eph. 2:8-9). People say "that nothing is sure in life but death and taxes"! If you make the Rapture, (1 Thess. 4:16-18) death is not sure; taxes are another issue altogether (Dan. 11:20)!

"**So he drew off his shoe**" People say "you never know what a man has been through unless you have walked a mile in his shoes!" I guess the nearer kinsman can put this theory to test; if the shoe fits, then he can wear it. If not, I guess he deposits it in the bank or uses it for a candy dish or some kind of knick knack to grow a flower in or something.

9 And Boaz said unto the elders, and *unto* all the people, Ye *are* witnesses this day, that I have bought all that *was* Elimelech's, and all that *was* Chilion's and Mahlon's, of the hand of Naomi.

    "witnesses" 2 Cor. 13:1b states "In the mouth of two or three witnesses shall every word be established". Boaz is making sure that everyone knows "this thing was not done in a corner" (Acts 26:26).

    "I have bought all" As mentioned in Ch. 2, redemption is to buy back something. Ruth, like us, was sold under sin (Rom. 7:14) and has been bought back. This event pictures Christ's atonement on the cross. Jesus purchased us back from the wages of sin and death (Rom. 6:23) with His blood (Acts 20:28) into everlasting life (John 3:16).

10 Moreover Ruth the Moabitess, the wife of Mahlon, have I purchased to be my wife, to raise up the name of the dead upon his inheritance, that the name of the dead be not cut off from among his brethren, and from the gate of his place: ye *are* witnesses this day.

    "have I purchased" D.L. Moody[60] points out that since Boaz is a type of the Lord Jesus Christ, and the nearer kinsman lacked the qualifications to be the perfect kinsman redeemer, then Boaz was the appropriate person to "buy back" all that was in hock. Jesus is the "Lord of the Harvest", the near kinsman, supplier of wants, Redeemer of the inheritance, Man who gives rest, Wealthy kinsman and Bridegroom.

---

60 Moody, D.L. Notes From My Bible and Thoughts From My Library. Baker Book House, 1979, p.51.

The nearer kinsman only wanted that which would benefit him and not that which would mar his name. Boaz knew the possible consequences of "buying" back all that belonged to Elimelech and yet he was willing to suffer whatever ridicule or losses that may entail. Christ endured the Cross for the joy that was set before Him (Heb. 12:2).

11 And all the people that *were* in the gate, and the elders, said, *We are* witnesses. The LORD make the woman that is come into thine house like Rachel and like Leah, which two did build the house of Israel: and do thou worthily in Ephratah, and be famous in Bethlehem:

"like Rachel and like Leah" Rachel and Leah were Jacob's (Israel) two wives (Gen. 32:28). However, they were Gentiles. Like their aunt Rebekah (Isaac's wife), they were Syrians (Gen. 25:20).[61]

"Ephratah" Ephratah is the region of where Bethlehem was located, which is where Christ was born. So, Rachel and Leah did **"worthily"** by being Gentile women in the messianic line, (not godly line as Scofield calls it), whose heritage brings forth the Saviour of all mankind, who is famous and from Everlasting to Everlasting (Ps. 90:2-4).

12 And let thy house be like the house of Pharez, whom Tamar bare unto Judah, of the seed which the LORD shall give thee of this young woman.

"Pharez, whom Tamar bare unto Judah" Tamar was also a Gentile woman (Gen. 38:1-6) Rachel, Leah, Tamar, and Ruth are all Gentile women who married a Jew, thus picturing the Gentile Bride of Christ. God the Father has a Jewish wife and God the Son has a Gentile Bride (see notes on vs. 6). God is the God of the Jews and the Gentiles (Gal. 3:28).

---

61 (Ruckman Ruth Commentary 397).

13 So Boaz took Ruth, and she was his wife: and when he went in unto her, the LORD gave her conception, and she bare a son.

"went in unto her" The marriage is now consummated as flesh joins flesh. (see notes on Ch. 3:16).

"the LORD gave her conception, and she bare a son" The Lord controls conception by opening the womb (Gen. 29:31), or keeping it closed (Gen. 20:18). The Lord opened the wombs of these women who aforetime were closed: (1.) Hanna (1 Sam. 1), (2.) the Shunammite woman (2 Kings 4), (3.) Sarah (Gen. 21), (4.) Rachel (Gen. 30), (5.) Manoah's wife to bear Sampson (Judges 13), (6.) Rebekah (Gen. 25) and (7.) Elizabeth to bear John the Baptist (Luke 1).

Children are a blessing and gift from the Lord (Ps. 127:3); many people just take for granted that they will get married and have children. To the couples that cannot seem to bear children, conception is not taken for granted. When conception does not occur, sometimes couples will try all kinds of fertility methods, but unless the Lord opens the womb, they will not be successful.

14 And the women said unto Naomi, Blessed *be* the LORD, which hath not left thee this day without a kinsman, that his name may be famous in Israel.

"Blessed *be* the LORD" The Lord has brought Naomi full circle from being a destitute widow in Moab with no hope, lineage, or kinsman to becoming a grandmother in the "House of Bread". The Lord gave her a caring soul to comfort her and stay by her side with no real possibility of ever having a family again or maybe not even being welcomed back in Israel. Ruth, an outsider, has married a "rich" man, converted to worshipping the Lord instead of idols, and produced a child thus, realistically saving Naomi's life and obtaining a promising future for herself. The Lord truly is awesome, wonderful, and worthy!!! Amen!

15 And he shall be unto thee a restorer of *thy* life, and a nourisher of thine old age: for thy daughter in law, which loveth thee, which is better to thee than seven sons, hath born him.

"**restorer of *thy* life**" See comments on verse 14.

"**for thy daughter in law, which loveth thee, which is better to thee than seven sons**" Ruth has gained the respect of the whole community. Naomi was lost, and now she is found (Luke 15:32). The credit for her restoration is given to Ruth, who stood faithfully by her side instead of departing and taking care of herself like Orpah. Naomi has gone from apostasy in Moab to being restored, picturing the restoration of the Jews during the Millennium.

"**loveth thee**" Someone said "the definition of love is the sovereign preference of another over oneself". Love is not self-serving, but self-giving, self-sacrificing; Ruth loves Naomi and walked the walk to show it.

16 And Naomi took the child, and laid it in her bosom, and became nurse unto it.

"**and laid it in her bosom**" As a parent, I can relate to the joy and excitement that was experienced by the birth of this child. To hold a baby and gaze into their eyes as they grab your pointer-finger with their whole hand and just stare at you, is priceless. To smell the "new born baby smell" is right after the "new car smell" that we do not want to go away, but it does, eventually with the baby smell as they grow up much too quickly.

This baby, though, is much more than the obvious joy experienced by having a new born; this baby is nothing short of a miracle. This baby has made Naomi "legitimate" again, restored her image, and brings so much hope that is yet to be seen such as being in the "Messianic line" that brings Jesus into the world.

Naomi and Ruth were both widows. What if Ruth went back like Orpah and thought of herself instead of her aged mother-in-law? What if anything happened on the trip back to Israel from Moab? What if they were run off and not accepted? What if Ruth wanted a check and did not want to work? What if "her hap" landed her in another field other than Boaz? What if Boaz was interested in profit like the nearer kinsman and did not have a heart for marriage? What if Ruth could not take the heat and manual labor and quit?

On and on we could go, but the Lord had all this arranged and the plan unfolded accordingly. Can you look back on your life and see God's hand in all your circumstances?

17 And the women her neighbours gave it a name, saying, There is a son born to Naomi; and they called his name Obed: he *is* the father of Jesse, the father of David.

"And the women her neighbours gave it a name" Notice the neighbors name the baby not-Boaz, Ruth, or Naomi. Obed in Hebrew means "serving, worshipping".[62]

Also, notice that Ruth is not mentioned any further, but Naomi is. Dr. Paul Heaton[63] suggests that this may be because God is taking the emphasis off the Gentile body of Christ (Ruth) and moving back to the Jew (Naomi).

This would follow doctrinally in the Bible where God turns back to dealing with the Jew in the time of Jacob's trouble (The Tribulation) and the Millennium at the Rapture, after the fulness of the Gentiles be come in (Rom. 11:25).

Notice further, the book of Matthew heralds the King in Ch. Three, the Kingdom of Heaven's constitution if offered to the Jews in Ch. 5-7,

---

62 *behindthename.com/name/obed.*
63 (Heaton Ruth Commentary 73).

the healing and miracle credentials of the Messiah are demonstrated in Ch. 8-9, the Messiah is rejected Ch.12, Jesus turns from the Jews to the Gentiles in Ch. 15, and finally at the end of Ch. 15, Jesus returns to the Jews and feeds them in the wilderness.

Further, in the introduction of this commentary paper was stated one of the most important things about the book of Ruth; it traces the genealogy of the Messiah. This genealogy is a portion of the Messianic line (see Matt. 1:1-6). Dr. Ruckman[64] states the lineage of Christ is the whole reason for this love story. God gives all this attention to Ruth because she turns out to be the great-grandmother of David, and Christ is "The Son of David" (Matt. 22:42).

18 Now these *are* the generations of Pharez: Pharez begat Hezron,

19 And Hezron begat Ram, and Ram begat Amminadab,

20 And Amminadab begat Nahshon, and Nahshon begat Salmon,

21 And Salmon begat Boaz, and Boaz begat Obed,

22 And Obed begat Jesse, and Jesse begat David.

"the generations" Vs. 18-22 are genealogy verses-yea! Genealogies occur more times in the Bible than some major doctrines such as the virgin birth, the death, burial, and resurrection of the Lord Jesus Christ for example. Genealogies are considered by most people as unessential, boring information that can be read over very quickly, however; man is to live "by every word of God" (Luke 4:4). Unfortunately, this includes genealogies as well.

Dr. Ruckman[65] states, "If the reader is bored with this long list of names, let him never forget this basic truth: since "love" in the Bible is defined as a man's love for his son (the Law of First Mention-Gen. 22:1-2),

---

64 (Ruckman Ruth Commentary 401).
65 (Ruckman Reference Bible 593).

the Author of the Holy Bible is interested in His Son. Being interested in His Son, God almighty records anything connected with His Son. The vast lists on names you are reading, are more important to God than such names as Henry VIII, Peter the Great, Alexander the great, Caesar Augustus, Nero, Magellan, Charlemagne, Columbus, Bismarck, Napoleon, Mohammed, Buddha, and the Popes".

Sometimes a "gold nugget" can be gleaned even from a genealogy! Take for example Genesis chapter five where there is a list of names beginning in vs. 2 that continues to vs. 32. If we read the names in order they would appear in English as: Adam, Seth, Enos, Cainan, Mahalaleel, Jared, Enoch, Methuselah, Lamech, and ending with Noah. Nothing interesting at first glance, right?

However, Chuck Missler[66] states when the English names are translated into Hebrew, the rendering would be: Adam=Man, Seth=Appointed, Enos=Mortal, Cainan=Sorrow, Mahalaleel=The Blessed God, Jared=Shall come down, Enos=Teaching, Methuselah=His death shall bring, Lamech=despairing, Noah=Comfort. Still not that interesting, right?

Try putting the English translation words together like a sentence in the order they are given in the chapter and you get: Man Appointed Mortal Sorrow. The Blessed God Shall come down Teaching. His death shall bring Despairing (or) Comfort.

Man is appointed mortal sorrow (death 1 Cor. 15:22). The Blessed God (Jesus) shall come down (1 Tim. 3:16) teaching (Mark 1:22) and His death (1 Cor. 15:1-4) shall bring despairing (or) comfort. Depending if you accept or reject Jesus, then you will despair in hell or be comforted in heaven. Jesus is on every page in the Bible and every passage point to Him in some manner. So, God gets the glory even in a genealogy!

---

66 (Missler youtube.com/watch?v=SFTr53H9GIA).

Finally, Deut. 23:2 states "A bastard shall not enter into the congregation of the Lord; even to his tenth generation shall he not enter into the congregation of the Lord". Pharez was born from Tamar, Judah's daughter-in-law who deceived Judah to have him raise up a son in the place of her dead husband Er, and thus was a bastard. From Pharez to David is exactly ten generations.

David, one of the greatest types of Christ in the Bible, becomes a prophet, priest and king-as Jesus was and is. David enters the congregation of the Lord and begins His service at thirty years of age as Jesus did (Luke 3:23). Another interesting fact found in a seemingly mundane passage of a genealogy.

BIBLIOGRAPHY

Commentaries, Religious Dictionaries, and Bible Versions

Canne, Browne, Blayney, Scott and others, The Treasury of Scripture Knowledge, (Mclean, VA: MacDonald Publishing Company, 1982), p. 188.

Campbell, Edward F. Jr., Ruth, (New York, NY: Doubleday & Company, Inc., 1975), p. 3-4.

Chambers, Oswald. My Utmost for His Highest, (Belgium: Barbour and Company, Inc.1935), Jan 4.

Chambers, Oswald. My Utmost for His Highest, (Belgium: Barbour and Company, Inc.1935), June 26.

Habershon, Ada R. A Study of the Types, (Grand Rapids, MI: Kregel Publications, 1957), pp. 68,70.

Heaton, Paul. Ruth A Story of Devotion, Virtue and Love. Morris Publishing, 2003, p. 8.

Larkin, Clarence. The Greatest Book on Dispensational Truth in the World, (Glenside, Pa: Rev. Clarence Larkin Est.1920), pp. 172-173.

Moody, D.L. Notes From My Bible and Thoughts From My Library, (Grand Rapids: Baker Book House, 1979, p. 51.

Ruckman, Peter. The Christian's Handbook of Manuscript Evidence, (Palatka, Florida: Pensacola Bible Press 1970), p. 38.

Ruckman, Peter S. Matthew Commentary. BB Bookstore, 1978, p. 560.

Ruckman, Peter. Psalms Commentary Vol. 2, (Pensacola, Fl: BB Bookstore, 2002, pp. 1241-42.

Ruckman, Peter. The Ruckman Reference Bible (Pensacola, Fl. U.S.A.:BB Bookstore, 2009), p. 484.

Strong, James. Strong's Exhaustive Concordance of the Bible, (Iowa Falls, IA: World Bible Publishers, Inc.1991), #7327, p. 142.

Ruckman, Peter. Judges and Ruth Commentary, (U.S.A.: BB Bookstore, 2015), p. 326.

Non-Published Materials

Jeremiah, David. Turning Point Radio Program, 1995.

Knox, James. sermon, 2012.

Walker, David. Various sermons preached at Calvary Baptist Church, Monticello, Florida, 2009-2018.

Dictionaries and Other Secular Sources

abarim-publications.com/Meaning/Moab.html#.Ww4LjyAh2Uk.

behindthename.com/name/obed.

en.wikipedia.org/wiki/Boaz.

scionofzion.com/drinking.htm.

Webster, Noah. Webster's Dictionary 1828, (webstersdictionary1828.com/Dictionary/dearth)

biblehub.com/topical/o/orpah.htm.

Gipp, Sam. jesus-is-savior.com/Bible/1611_authorized_king_james.htm.

Chuck Missler youtube.com/watch?v=SFTr53H9GIA.

Audio

Estep, Greg. MD5078 Ruth, (CBBI Dayton, Oh: Audio Tape 10 vs19@118 minutes).

Hauenstein, Michael. MD5082 Typology, (CBBI Dayton, Oh: Audio Tape 1@12 minutes approx.).

THE HOLY GHOST

Everything written, remembered, and imagined!

Trust Publishers House,
the trusted name in quality Christian books.

Trust House Publishers
PO Box 3181
Taos, NM 87571

TrustHousePublishers.com